SIDELINES

FOUR DECADES OF SUNDAYS WITH "DA BEARS"

By:
Chet Ballard & Tom Ballard

With:
Marc Freden

This paperback first edition was published worldwide in 2023 by On The Marc Publishing.

Copyright © 2023 all rights reserved.

By Chet Ballard & Tom Ballard with Marc Freden.

All rights reserved. No part of this publication may be reproduced, distributed, or transmitted in any form or by any means, including photocopying, recording, or other electronic or mechanical methods, without the prior written permission of the publisher, except in the case of brief quotations embodied in critical reviews and certain other noncommercial uses permitted by copyright law.

ISBN-13: 979-8-9889123-0-9

Library of Congress Control Number: 2023914903

For permission requests, write to the publisher, addressed "Attention: Permissions Coordinator," at the address below:

sidelineschicagobook@gmail.com

ACKNOWLEDGEMENTS

None of this adventure would have happened if it not for an inspired proposition by *Frank McGurk*…better known as our **Uncle Fran.** This book is dedicated to him.

From Chet:

- I always wanted a Superbowl ring but got something better, a wedding ring, from the love of my life Sharon who has been with me through the Bears years to this book's tears. None of which could have been done without her.
- I have to acknowledge the constant support of my family and the memory jogs from my close friends, many of whom were there along with my current co-workers who have been overwhelmingly encouraging through this process.
- I must thank James Messer for his book cover design and his lovely wife Toula Mavridou Messer for her insight and motivation.
- A special thank you goes out to Danilo Rubias who connected us to our collaborator.

ACKNOWLEDGMENTS

From Tom:

- It doesn't get better than sharing your life and adventures with someone who cares and wants to be there with you every step of the way. I have to thank my son Tommy for growing up with me.
- You don't go through this without making some lasting friends. I've been blessed with more than my fair share…and certainly, too many to mention. You know who you are and what you mean.
- To my family who are with me on a much deeper level than even they may know. You know what I would say to you if you were here with me right now.
- And to God above who has been a force in my life through this entire experience and continues to be alongside me each and every day.

Finally, we'd both like to give a heartfelt and much-appreciated thank you to Marc Freden who was able to spin cocktail party anecdotes and "sidelines" into the stories we were wanting and meant to tell.

TABLE OF CONTENTS

Introduction	1
TAILGATE	7
Preface	9
KICK-OFF	17
He Made Me an Offer	19
FIRST DOWN	33
"Da Bears"	35
Chicago	41
I Didn't Sign Up for This	51
Just Between Us Guys	61
Silence is Golden	69
Those Were the Days	75
There's No Place Like Home	81
SECOND DOWN	91
Mining for Gold	93
Eavesdropping	101
There's No Crying in Football	109
Damned if You Did	117
Paranoia Can Destroy Ya	123
Up in Smoke	131
The Fog of War	135
Some Players Can Be Real D*cks	141

THIRD DOWN — 145

- They Sign Your Checks — 147
- Holier Than Thou — 159
- Passing the Buck — 165
- Just One of the Guys — 171
- Behind Every Great Man — 183
- Seeing Red — 193
- Second Generation — 197
- From Players…to People…to Pals — 205
- You'd Think They Don't Notice — 215
- The Doctor is In — 221

FOURTH DOWN — 225

- You Can't Always Get Away with It — 227
- Photobombing — 235
- The One That Got Away — 243
- The Ultimate Loss — 247
- Limo Service — 251
- Take A Deep Breath — 259
- Going Low…After Mile High — 271

TOUCHDOWN — 275

- Was It Worth It — 277

POST GAME WRAP UP — 285

- But I'm a Fan Too — 287

INTRODUCTION

Chicago in the early '80s. Some would say it was grittier, dirtier, and more dangerous than it is today. But was it? It was just a different time, with a different standard of living. Sure, you had the extremes of the urban jungle known as Cabrini Green. But then you had comfortable housing with rents hovering around $200 a month in the inner city. Touch that today!

There were high points such as the expansion of the "El" public transportation from the north side to the south side. The first female Mayor, Jane Byrne—a progressive thinker and doer who succumbed to sexism and misogyny—to the election of the first black mayor, Harold Washington. And by 1983, the first cell phones arrived in Chicago at a cost of $4000 each. Oh, and by the way, that same year, Chicago experienced forty-nine inches of snow.

But about this time, Chicago was also gaining some national attention—notoriety, both good and bad. The 1980 blockbuster movie, "The Blues Brothers", starring John Belushi and Dan Aykroyd, was shot completely in Chicago and made the windy city "cool." The arts, in their own right, were getting attention. Second City, Steppenwolf Theater, and Hubbard Street Dance Company were all gaining national attention and the aptly named artist Judy Chicago put the gallery scene on the map with her iconic piece "The Dinner Party."

But notoriety comes in different forms. Plenty of people remember Spiderman who, in 1981, climbed down the Sears Tower—then reaching 110 floors and was the tallest building in the world—and the John Hancock building, using just suction cups and sky hooks. He claimed it wasn't a publicity stunt but rather a call to action for a potential safety option in escaping from architectural towers in times of crisis.

And speaking of crisis, in 1982, Chicago alarmed the nation when seven people died from cyanide-laced Tylenol bought over the counter at local drug stores. That incident changed the over-the-counter drug safety packaging as we know it today. You could say, Chicagoans gave their lives, so millions of Americans live safely today.

Two people getting national attention were the darlings of the field and the court. In 1982, running back Walter Payton was catching the eye of fans and the nation when had a record year with the Bears. And another notable newcomer was a 1984 draft pick for the Chicago Bulls named Michael Jordan. It wasn't long before, these two, their respective teammates, and the city itself made Chicago the focal point for national sports interest.

If the beginning of the 80s seemed a lot for the windy city…don't worry…by 1986 everyone could collectively take a day off. "Ferris Bueller's Day Off", the national exhale of a movie starring Matthew Broderick, was filmed right there in the heart of the city.

Why were the early to mid-eighties so special to us? Because that is when life changed in the biggest, best possible way. The Ballard brothers and the Bears became a four-decade winning combination.

So, who are we, Chet and Tom Ballard, who grew up with Chicago as part of our backyard? We weren't a couple of hapless "Joes" who simply landed a golden ticket. Were we given an opportunity? You betcha! Have we taken advantage of that opportunity every step of the way? As best we could! Did we deserve it? Not more than others. But, we feel, it's what we did with the opportunity we were handed that made our lives a great adventure.

From the very start of our respective times with Andy Frain—our actual employer who placed us at Soldier Field and with the Bears organization—we became collectors: of moments, of memorabilia, of adventures, of anecdotes…of everything. And we would do almost anything to add to that collection. We were moving through the job at hand, never forgetting how the privilege and prestige of even being on the periphery with the greats of the game would mean to those who would or could never be at arms distance to the action—both personal and professional. It was and always is a vicarious adventure on par with lucid dreaming.

It wasn't so much a job as it was and has been an addiction. We both had separate careers that sustained us. But the weekends, the games, they are what fed us. They were the little something on the side that hooked us.

Oh, there were others along for the ride: co-workers, cohorts, and coconspirators who have chosen to and not to participate in rattling our memories as to the comings and goings of our misadventures only to find us ending up telling our side of the story as the way we saw it, interpreted it, or experienced it. There's no dispute in the facts, the events, or the participants.

So how do we go about telling our story? Certainly not from one perspective. Although there are Chet's stories that are uniquely his and there are Tom's stories that are individually his experiences. And on several occasions, despite having different assignments and responsibilities within the organization, our paths and opportunities crossed, and we shared the moment. We will attribute our individual contributions to the storytelling with a simply named notation at the end of the passage:

--Chet

(For a Chet contribution)

Or

--Tom

(For a Tom contribution)

This book is not a chronicle or a history. It's an insightful and thought provoking, fun romp by a couple of guys who may have had more access than common sense at times. It is an entertainment portfolio of anecdotal moments from two brothers—the only brothers with four decades of behind-the-scenes access—who carved out a unique, one-of-a-kind, unprecedented situation that put them in the right places at the right time on a weekly basis, literally being paid to be the super-fans we already were.

We could have stood our post, done our job, observed nothing, and watched the game. But where's the fun in that?

2 Brothers

4 Decades

1 Fantastic Ride

Now they're telling their…

SIDELINES!

PREFACE

Who was I to be standing there, staring? I shouldn't have been there. I knew I shouldn't. But there was no one to stop me. I had done the job I was assigned, and it's not that my time was my own, but it was just that I had nowhere to be. And, moreover, no one really watched what I did…as long as I did the job that was expected. It was strange to have that kind of autonomy. I was a kid, after all, and this was my first job ever. Maybe, I didn't know better. Maybe my bosses just trusted me. I came and went as I wanted, within reason, like I owned the stadium. I wasn't cocky… just naïve.

My formal assignment was to usher the visiting coaches to their box high above the stadium field. That's what I do. I am an Andy Frain employee—Chicago's prestigious valet/usher/security company. Being an Andy Frain employee was not only a good job but a competitive and sought-after position. I was lucky to be there as a young teen, dressed in my blue blazer adorned with its gold trimmings, blue pants with matching gold length-long striping, blue cap, and white gloves. We looked military grade important, no matter what the position—almost too formal for a stadium setting. But in Chicago, when you saw an Andy Frain presence, you saw quality employees, service, and a tight-run ship.

The Chicago Bears games were my Sunday routine. As an Andy Frain employee, you were allowed to choose your assignments as the company had contracts with event venues all over the city. I always made sure my assignments included Sunday Bears games because, like most Chicagoans, I was a fan. Imagine getting paid for being at the game. That's what I thought about. Whatever the responsibility that came with it was secondary.

You didn't arrive in your uniform. You changed in the official Andy Frain locker room. If I didn't feel formally part of the Bears organization, just knowing that we had an official locker room let me, at least, feel we were part of the bigger picture. The uniform was precise, and faces were expected to be shaved. Once readied, we then reported to Jim McKittrick who had the assignment slips. McKittrick cut a formidable swath. All of six foot five and close to three hundred pounds, he was as intimidating as he was large. It was intimidation by reputation. Yes, he ran the entire Andy Frain organization at the stadium—nothing happened without his approval, and nothing got past him—but he was also a Chicago police officer, and I for one wasn't about to take any of that on.

Once at the stadium, there were plenty of jobs to be had. Yet, there was little say as to who was assigned to what. It was McKittrick's say only. You got your assignment slip during the process of the roll call.

McKittrick sized you up, chose your placement, and sent you on your way. There was no second-guessing or backtalk. You did as you were told.

Originally, I was assigned to the track high above the stands to guard a quadrant against people jumping the streetside gates, making their way up the stairs, and inevitably sneaking into the game. Although I was just a teen myself, I was a big kid and most people assumed I was much older and far more intimidating than I really was. Ironically, I let more of my friends jump the gate than I ever stopped strangers from getting in but that was just a perk, in my teen mind, of having been given the keys to the kingdom.

By season three, my job responsibilities had advanced through a matter of circumstances, and I was permanently assigned to escorting the visiting coaches to their sky boxes upon their arrival and then to the locker room at half-time, back again, and then back down after the game. It would seem easy enough. But these were important people and fans weren't always fantastic. Despite that Andy Frain had a security department, I was defacto, acting as an usher, security, and butler to their needs.

I liked this position. I got to meet some of the best of the best in the game. And when I say meet…they sometimes threw me a comment, held brief conversations, or asked my opinion. Other times, I was invisible. So be it. I was seventeen years old and no friends of mine had a job like mine. It was hard not to be in awe, even a little, of the position I was in.

Now when I say I was taking these V.I.P.'s to their coach's box, don't imagine the suites of today. Back then, they were simply a box. Picture a square room painted a monotonous Bear's blue with a couple of lines of tiered seating like those you would find in a cinema or theater, a table or two, and a bar across the back for refreshments. It was nothing glamorous, just functional. And it was cold in the winter. Insulation and double-paned glass were luxuries yet to be.

Old Soldier Field at the time was designed like a colosseum. Tall, ancient-looking columns lined the east and west sides of the stadium, the exterior was a stone edifice and the stairs up to the bleacher seating were wide, stone, numerous, and unwieldy for those out of shape. While the look of the stadium was both impressive and intimidating—an icon for the era—it took some work schlepping those coaches up and down from the box to the locker room. I quickly understood why they would need an escort. The slog up the stairs meant the coaches were vulnerable to the fans, who, as I said, were not always fantastic. If they recognized the coaches, there could be cheers and jeers, harassment, and all kinds of name-calling. The visiting coaches didn't have the luxury of inside passage to the box. They essentially had to run the gauntlet of the stairs and it was my job to get them up there and into the box expediently.

I got the coaches safely and securely to the box, asked politely if they needed anything while I was there, and with nothing left to do until half-time, I excused myself.

The problem I always had at this point in my day was where I would physically go in the downtime. Many times, I simply stayed in the coach's box under the guise of being available for their needs. Sometimes, I went down to the field. And let me tell you there is nothing like the sound and sights from the sidelines. Other times, I would simply wander until I found a comfortable spot to stand and watch the game. Suffice it to say, I had time on my hands.

But on this particular day, I was excited. The new president was there. Michael McCaskey—the heir apparent to the ownership of the team. It was his first game at the stadium, and I was determined to get an eye on him. This guy was tantamount to God in my seventeen-year-old eyes. How does anyone run a football team? It was a concept someone my age could barely wrap his head around. I was just happy to be in the stadium. Run a football organization? Incomprehensible!

So how did this guy become the head of the Bears? Without making this a history lesson, the Halas family owned the Bears since its origins. George Halas Sr. was determined to create a Halas/Bears dynasty and keep the team a Halas legacy for time in memorial. To that end, he groomed his son George "Mugsy" Halas to inherit the team when the time was right. His plan was simple—always leave the team to a Halas male so the Halas name would always be associated with the team. But the best-laid plans don't always come to fruition. Mugs died in 1979 at fifty-four years old from a heart attack leaving George Sr. alive and in a predicament. Mugsy's wife it turned out subsequently sold her inherited shares in the team outside of the family. So, when the time was right, the last remaining Halas descendant was Virginia, now Halas McCaskey. Virginia may be the owner, but someone had to run the day-to-day business of the business. Enter Michael McCaskey in 1983.

I made my way to the owner's box. Again, as an Andy Frain, bedecked in my military-style uniform, no one would question me being there.

The box was on the top level and had a small glass window in the door through which I could see. Again, it was nothing glamorous with the exception of refreshments already lined on the bar stretching across the back wall and there was a formally uniformed female box attendant to serve those, inside. As I mentioned, the seating was perfunctory and the color bland—again, a far cry from the luxury of today's suites.

The box was not crowded, Virginia McCaskey was there, chatting with a few presumed guests. Michael McCaskey sat at the far end of the row of seats. He was a distinguished-looking man. Young and formal, wearing a suit—the uniform of owners and presidents in the era—and his hair just so. He was the very definition of a banker which was appropriate as his background I was to find out was in finance.

McCaskey, it turns out, has a formidable resume in finance—an alumnus of Weatherhead School of Management at Case Western Reserve University and taught at the business schools of UCLA and Harvard. I was a sports geek, and those credentials were lost on me when it comes to the running of a sports team. It would take me years to understand that a team is a business and that this sport is anything but a game.

I couldn't help but notice that McCaskey wasn't paying much attention to the game. He was, though, paying close attention to the man next to him and the notepad within a portfolio upon which that man was scribbling. Needless to say, I had no idea who that man was and, from my vantage point behind the glass, had no idea what they were saying. But I could see that the man was jotting down X's and O's all over the page. I was intrigued by the interaction. It seemed like doodling more than writing. But he would point to the page and turn to McCaskey and speak. McCaskey would nod and sometimes comment. I watched for some time as no one questioned why I was there and, moreover, no one in the box seemed to notice my peeping.

After a while, the female attendant came out of the box and darted past me. I stopped her just long enough to ask her a question being careful of my phrasing. There was an understanding that you simply didn't speak about the McCaskeys and certainly nothing negative or you would be fired. And it was further thought that there were spies all around the stadium baiting the employees with questions like: "Hey, how do you think the McCaskeys are doing with the team?" Again, if you said something negative, you were out. It was understood, the box attendants were most probably some of those spies. So, with more curiosity than trepidation, I stopped the attendant.

"Excuse me, do you know who the man is who is sitting with Mr. McCaskey?"

She turned to me and answered abruptly, "His coach."

"His coach?" I continued wondering what he could possibly need a coach for.

"Yes," she added, itching to move on, "He is explaining the game to Mr. McCaskey. Mr. McCaskey doesn't know anything about football."

My jaw dropped as she turned and walked away. Was she right? Could she really be giving me this kind of insider information? How could the new president of the Bears not know the fundamentals of football but be in charge of everything from selecting players to a general manager? This is an incredible piece of information that I, unfortunately, could share with no one for fear of losing my job. We're sunk, I thought.

Later, I was to find out that McCaskey attended Yale where he lettered in football. Still, the attendant had said what she said. Could she have been baiting me for a negative reaction, putting my job in jeopardy, or was she correct on a different level? He may have known how to play football but what did he know about running a football organization? In that sense my original thoughts were valid. If he doesn't know what he is doing…on any level…we're sunk.

Was I in the wrong place at the right time or the right place at the wrong time? As a fan, I couldn't believe what I was hearing. As an employee, I couldn't believe I was there to hear it. And it made me wonder… just how did I get here?

--Chet

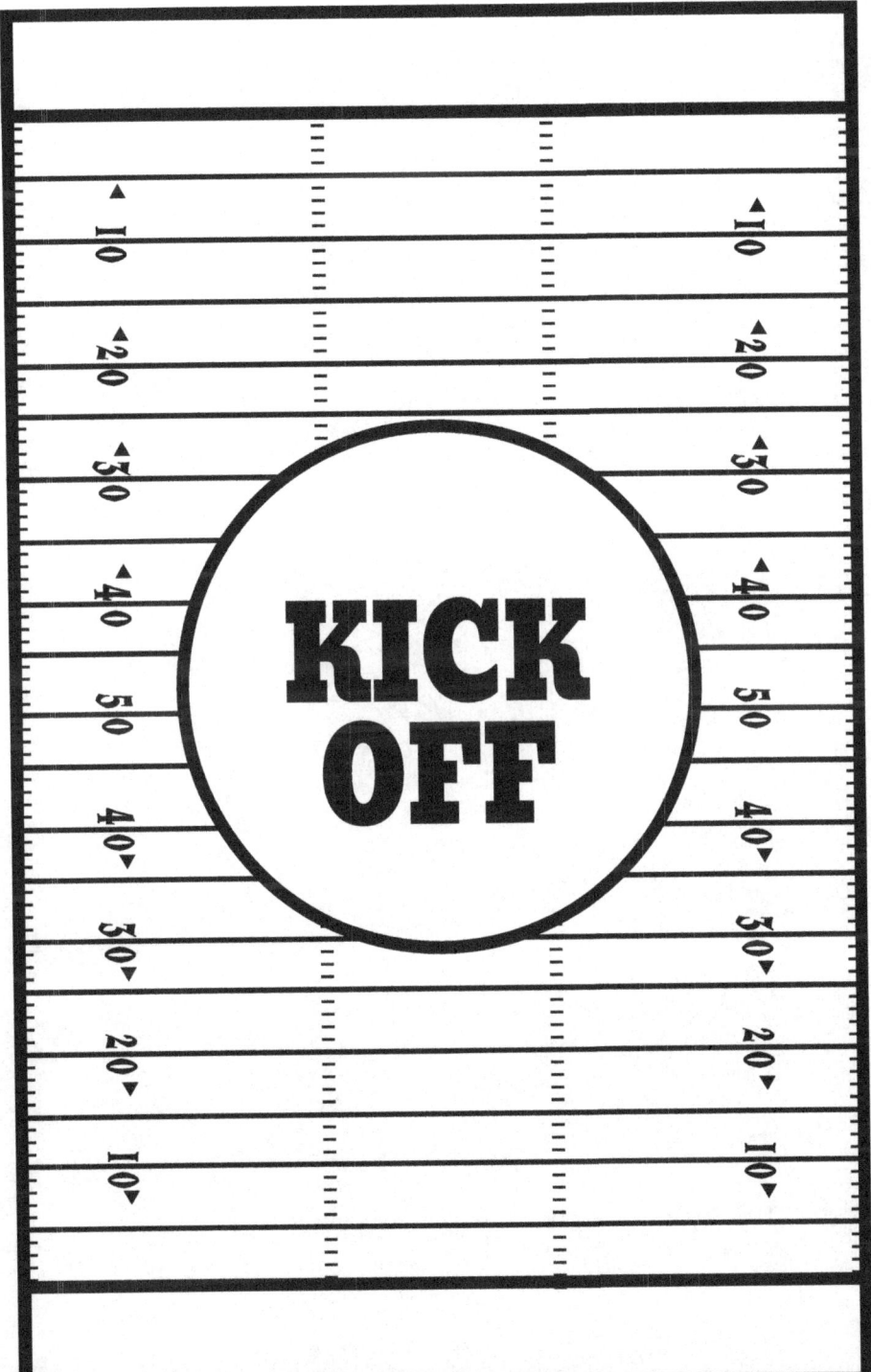

HE MADE ME AN OFFER I COULDN'T REFUSE!

Everyone knew Frank McGurk. A banker by trade for much of his professional life and later a board member for a company called Gas City. As I understood it, he went around greater Chicago and negotiated the land purchase for various gas stations. But under his auspice, I was sure there were other dealings he had his hands in. He seemed to have his hands in everything. But that was not the only reason why people knew him and liked him. He was simply "that" guy. At just six feet tall, he seemed to stand even taller as he commanded the room. Moreover, he was gregarious and charismatic, with James Caan, movie star good looks and sang like Sinatra. I don't remember him ever not dressed impeccably—mostly in suits, sometimes just a suit jacket, but always dapper for the occasion. He was the guy who bought all the drinks. And the drinking was a skill he was good at—enjoyed his beer, with a gut to prove it. And I was proud to call him my uncle.

As a boy, I spent many weekends with Uncle Frank, Fran as we knew him, and he was generous with his time. He took us, my brother and I, to spend most weekends with him and my aunt. As a regular treat, we went to many sporting events of all kinds: Blackhawks games, Notre Dame games, you name it…afterward hanging out at the bars where he held court. That's where he shone. Later in my teens, I was a big kid and looked older for my age. So, on more than a few occasions, I shared a beer with Uncle Fran and the guys and blended in as if I belonged.

If it weren't for Uncle Fran and one of our sporting forays, I probably would not have gotten my initial introduction to the Andy Frain gentlemen. Even at a young age, I thought of them as gentlemen because that's the way they presented…as gentlemen in the crowd while corralling the crowd. They were impressive, with their royal blue uniforms, white shirts, ties, white gloves, and brimmed hats. Yes, more military than valet but they commanded respect—certainly, around the city and, definitely mine.

For anyone who has never heard of Andy Frain, the company was founded in 1924 out of sheer frustration. Mr. Frain was an entrepreneur who saw the perpetual gate crashing at Chicago Stadium hockey games as an unacceptable nuisance and suggested professional ushers would create an air of authority to stem the problem. It worked. And it wasn't long before that recipe for success caught the eye of William Wrigley Jr. of the namesake Wrigley Field who became so impressed with the service that he invested enough money to provide the now iconic uniforms for which Andy Frain employees are known. Over a very short amount of time, Andy Frain ushers were in demand and quickly became a symbol of security, decorum, and formality at events both personal and professional. Over the years, Andy Frain branched out from sports to concert venues to special events and now boasts branches in forty-five locations throughout the country.

So, one afternoon, most likely after a game, presumably over a beer and definitely out of the blue, Uncle Fran asks me if I would like to be one of those Andy Frain gentlemen. Sure, I thought but doubted it was ever going to be. I was just 14 years old, underaged to work, didn't have a driver's license, let alone a car to get me to and back and, yeah, did I mention, I was just 14 years old and underaged? That didn't seem to deter Uncle Fran in the least. And why he thought I needed a job at just 14 years old is still a mystery to me to this day. At my size and height, and with the occasional beer in my hand to blend in, I certainly wasn't curbing his style at the bar.

"Let me handle the age problem," he assured, promising me a doctored identification. He knew somebody. He always knew somebody. In fact, he also knew somebody at Andy Frain who would look the other way at the doctored documents and allow me to jump the waiting list for the much-in-demand Andy Frain jobs. This wasn't like I was being sneaked in as a soda jerk or an attendant for one of Uncle Fran's gas station cronies. This was Andy Frain. It was the big time. And frankly, I was amazed he was pulling it off. But that was Uncle Fran. He just always knew somebody.

And faster than I could say "Okay…but…" I was in the door and be-suited in one of those fine-tailored, almost costume-like uniforms I had so admired from afar. At 14 years old, I was an official Andy Frain representative.

Don't get me wrong, working for Andy Frain wasn't far off being in the military. They were and are a precision-based organization. It is their way or the highway. Even though they were virtually the only game in town, they lived by their white-gloved reputation for excellent service—no matter what the venue, no matter what the occasion. The uniforms were a symbol. The man wearing it carried the reputation.

What made the job instantly magical was that I could actually choose where I wanted to work. Andy Frain had contracts with venues all over the city and beyond. On your weekly work request sheet, you could simply ask for the venue in which you wanted to be placed. There were no guarantees but for the most part, you went where you asked to go. I consistently wrote down that I wished to be placed at Soldier Field and work with the legendary Bears. But, of course, the devil is in the details, and I was never quite sure if the jig would be up when it came for me to fill in the section which asked for my driver's license number, whether I had a car or reliable transportation and the like. All of which, I didn't have… not at my age. But week after week, Sunday after Sunday, I found myself at Soldier Field facing one of Chicago's finest, the aforementioned Officer McKittrick, the head of Andy Frain operations at the field, to get my in-stadium weekly assignment.

I was a big guy, certainly for my age, and I was assigned to the top tier of the stadium and guarding my quadrant's gate to assure there would be no gate crashing from eager fans looking for free entry to the game.

The job was relatively simple: patrolling the perimeter and guarding the gate. And when I say guarding the gate, I say that with a healthy wink of the eye because, on many Sundays, friends and acquaintances benefited from my ability to turn a blind eye to their ticketless entre through my gate at my discretion. It was as simple as organizing a time to meet and me giving them the all-clear. It was up to them to scramble to find empty seats and lay low. One regular benefactor was my brother Tom.

This went on for two years until two factors changed my life: fried chicken and NFL security—and the two aren't mutually exclusive.

Let me start with the chicken. Brown's chicken. It was an unremarkable local chain of fried chicken joints that dotted the city. It came into my life because Brown's chicken catered the lunches for the coaches and other V.I.P.s throughout the stadium. Now the fun begins.

Not everyone who was entitled to the boxed lunch of chicken cared to eat the chicken and it fast became a scramble among others as to who would end up with the leftover boxes.

I know it seems petty but the Brown's chicken and who ended up with it was an issue during every game. It was an issue, so much so, that over time, I even knew enough to get word to the caterer to order extra boxes for non-existent V.I.P.s just to service the demands of say the cops and the crew who grew to expect a box lunch, deserving or not.

And one man who loved his Brown's chicken boxed lunch was the head of NFL security—that's ALL of NFL security in Chicago—George Mandich. Picture, if you will a Peter Sellers, Pink Panther, doppelganger, and you will get a fairly good idea of the image of Mr. Mandich. He wore the same blue suit, black tie, and a London Fog trench coat. He wore that every Sunday, every week, every season, every year that I knew him.

And this is how Brown's Chicken and NFL security collide to change my life for the good, for the better.

One Sunday, Mandich comes charging up the stairs looking rather menacing. He points at me, and

> **A REAL PISSING MATCH!**
>
> Well, this chicken became a matter of mystery, and wouldn't you know I would find myself right in the middle of it.
>
> On one particular Sunday, I was approached by two of Chicago's finest who felt slighted that one of Andy Frain's senior supervisors was helping himself to the leftover chicken before they had a chance to get a grab at it. Just being a teenager and no jurisdiction over the abandoned boxes or the supervisor's actons, I was left with no response. But they sure had one.
>
> They told me that they were going to teach him a lesson for not knowing his place and they were going to take a box of chicken, piss it and then hand it to him for him to unwittingly eat. And they did.
>
> Some weeks went by, and I hadn't seen the older supervisor at the Stadium, and I began to ask around. I was told that after that Sunday, he had taken ill and eventually died. I was shocked! Had the pissed chicken killed this man?
>
> I let the officers know what had happened and it seemed suspicious that he'd gotten sick just after their little prank. And then I judiciously walked away.
>
> To this day, I still wonder what happened to that man. I know he was older. I know they pissed in the box. But I never really trusted that chicken either.

the guy standing next to me and says that he needs one of us for a special assignment.

The back story to this special assignment involved the former head coach of the Bears from the early 70s, Abe Gibron who was now at the Tampa Bay Buccaneers. It seems the last time the Bears and the Buccaneers met at Soldier Field things didn't go well for old Abe. Getting from the coach's box on the visitor's side to the locker room at halftime meant that Gibron would have to walk down the ninety-seven stairs through the fans to get there. Gibron is not a small man—rotund is a nice way to put it. So, while laboriously making his way down the stairs, he was spotted, heckled, and pelted with food and debris. The long and short of the exchange was that Abe filed a complaint with the NFL stating the Bears had the worst security in the league and if it wasn't fixed, he would not allow Tampa Bay to come back to Chicago.

The complaint was taken very seriously which led Mandich to look into my young eyes like an FBI agent and start barking to me and my sidekick that he wants one of us to wait outside the coaches' box at halftime, escort the coach down to the locker room, wait there until halftime is over and escort him back up to the box. Seemed simple enough. Without much hesitation, the guy next to me puts up his hand and says he'll do it. Once Mandich is reassured that the assignment is understood and will be taken care of, he retreats to find…of all things…some Brown's chicken. (Actually, it was the coleslaw; I had the unnerving privilege of watching him gulp and slobber on several occasions which he scooped with his bare hands or ate straight from the container, letting plenty of it run down the side of his face. Quite the undignified show. But there was something about those boxed lunches that brought out the crazy in people.)

As soon as Mandich left, my buddy turned to me and said that he didn't really want to do the assignment. What he really wanted was…you guessed it…to fight for a box of Brown's chicken. Again, I don't know what the attraction is to that chicken, but I let him at it and I took over the security assignment despite technically being just an usher.

The next game came with the same assignment. And as I was waiting for the coaches by the locker room at halftime, Mandich came by.

"Listen, you're my guy," he began. "You're going to do this job every single week from now on. I am going to talk to Jim McKittrick and tell him you're my guy."

From that moment on, and I would like to thank the fine folks at Brown's Chicken for their part, I had it made. Rather than standing guard with a wink and nod as my friends and brother jumped the gate for freebee seats, I officially would be walking the greats of the game down what is known as Bear's Alley—from the arrival gate, to and past the necessary locker rooms, and on to the visiting coaches' box. And in the meantime, I would be free to wander, explore, invent, and reinvent myself as something great. Because what I learned in short order was that proximity to the bigwigs made me a bigwig by proxy. And I, at just 17 years old was going to take as much advantage of that as I possibly could. My secret weapon was the coaches themselves. If I was ever in a place where

I shouldn't be, I simply said I was on call for a coach, waiting for a coach, at the coach's disposal and no one ever questioned me.

To that end, it wasn't long before I thought to myself if I was being thought of as important and above the fray, then perhaps I should have something that distinguishes me from the fray. The Andy Frain uniform included a white-brimmed hat, the style matching the kind you would see on a street police officer. Mine was no different from anyone else's. And that is when I came up with the idea to distinguish myself.

205 West Madison Street, Chicago, was the address of the Superior Uniform Cap Company. So, when I walked in unannounced and without the authority to be sized for a new cap that would be emblazoned with the single title of CHIEF written across the front, you would have thought someone...anyone...would have questioned who I was and had any of a number of realistic questions as to why they should be making my hat. They didn't. The hat was made, delivered, and I wore it. No one questioned the title change—not my fellow employees and, more importantly, not my bosses. Now I really had the keys to the kingdom. I just had to keep them under my hat...so to speak.

Word got to me some years later that back at the Andy Frain headquarters a man named Jack McDonald would refer to me as the guy who has the job that everyone at Andy Frain wants. I was even eventually introduced to the big guy himself, Mr. Frain, as that person. It was all very funny to me because as time went on, I was simply making up the rules as I went along: respecting what I had to do, all the while doing what I wanted to do. This is why the only title I truly appreciated, was thankful for and answered to, was a title I held for two decades which was as made up as many of my job responsibilities: MAYOR OF BEARS ALLEY.

--Chet

Uncle Fran drank, that's for sure. So much so, that it was a precarious drive to Chicago on the weekends he picked up Chet and me for a city visit. It was nothing for him to down a case of beer in a relatively short amount of time and still nothing for him to get behind the wheel afterward. My parents were nervous when he would show up a little shaky and unbalanced, but nothing was ever said. There were obvious cringes. But it was Uncle Fran and somehow, it would all work out. It was important for Uncle Fran and my Aunt Marion to have us for the weekends as they didn't have any children of their own and we filled in a palpable void. For my parents, it gave them a rest. My father worked six days a week both at the Mercantile Exchange and as an engineer with the railroad. They could use the break.

I am six years older than my brother, so I was the built-in babysitter as we hopped from bar to bar as Uncle Fran mastered the art of the schmooze with influential cronies with ties to the Blackhawks and the Bears among others. He would palm me a fist full of quarters and we would find our way to the foosball table or arcade games in the back of the room where I could take care of a very young Chet while Uncle Fran held court "doing business."

I was too young to completely understand but the judges, attorneys, and other influential people he would meet with were all about cutting deals for the gas company where Fran worked. The company was looking to secure retail, food, and liquor licenses for the different locations that Fran had already picked out, mostly in distressed neighborhoods where grocery stores were hard to find—looking to create the early equivalent of the modern convenience store gas stations of today.

Among those "business partners" were people with season tickets to the various home teams, and, on many occasions, we were the beneficiaries of those tickets. To say they were generous with those tickets was an understatement. On many occasions, we could be handed as many as eight or ten tickets at a time and I could bring all my buddies. Let's face it, I was in my teens at the time, and this was a fairly impressive deal amongst my friends. Good times!

By the time Chet was in his teens and I was no longer playing the babysitter role, I had moved on a bit from those weekends with Uncle Fran. I was dating my high school sweetheart who would later become my wife. But I still loved going to the games. So, when Chet got the job with Andy Frain, he became my ticket in. And if you are wondering how getting me in worked, here goes:

We would set up a time on a call during the day when I should meet him at the V.I.P. entrance just off to the side of the general ticket holder entrance at the front of the stadium. If I missed the time or he couldn't be there for some reason, the situation was a bust and I was not going to get in. There was security there: checking passes, tickets, and credentials if you were part of the media. I had none of the aforementioned. I couldn't linger indefinitely without a bona fide reason for standing there or again, I would be questioned, have no answers, therefore the situation would be a bust and I would not be getting in. Inevitably, Chet would be at the gate, looking very official with his Andy Frain uniform, to have a few words with the security gentleman at the gate, indicating who I was to give me the okay. Chet would leave at that point. There was no fraternization or anything to make it look like this was anything but a professional interplay. Everyone was careful not to tip off anyone. And for the record, for as many times as it happened, there were plenty when it couldn't happen, and we all understood. That's simply the way things went.

It was a pretty good system until the one game when I could have blown the whole deal.

It was the 1985-86 season, and the Bears were playing the Packers. The rivalry between these two teams was intense. Who wouldn't want to see this game? I was newly married and, as the Bears had become "the" national team to watch, the ticket prices were insane. Chet, once again, made the magic happen and I was in…but with nowhere to sit. I had a field pass. So, I stood…in of all places…along the Bears' sideline between the thirty-yard lines, where only players and team personnel were meant to be. It's called the bench area and I prayed that I would just blend in, and no one would confront me as to what I was doing there. For much of the game, everything went fine.

As it happened, for this game, the quarterback, Randy Wright, was out on the injured list and the backup quarterback was playing the game. He wasn't particularly good and during one play, he threw a wayward pass. Wayward sure. But caught nonetheless…by me.

Chet was in the coaches' box with the Packers' coaches and to my understanding sees the pass go down from high above. He was apoplectic with fear. This was a nationally televised football game and there I am standing with the caught pass on the sidelines on which I am not supposed to be standing.

"Throw it back," he is screaming to me as if I could hear. He was more in fear of being caught than I…and I can assure you, I was worried.

The rule is to throw the ball back to the referee and let the game progress. Now, as a serious memorabilia collector in the making, nothing would have made me happier than to hang on to that ball. But all eyes were on me. I saw the ref approach and then stood there waiting. After what seemed to be an eternity of time, I did the right thing and tossed back the ball and waited for my fate…to be tossed from the field. Still, no one questioned who the nobody was who caught the ball and, moreover, what was he doing in the restricted area.

That kind of luck wore out that season.

The Bears had won the Super Bowl and security was at an all-time high. There were no more wink-and-nod passes after 1985 and it was suggested if I wanted to see the games up close and personal, to follow in the family's footsteps and get a job with Andy Frain. It hadn't occurred to me at that point. I had a successful career in radio sales and doing this on the side wasn't on my radar. But Chet had the legacy connection, and I did love the action.

Just as ushering was Chet's beat, security became mine. Ironic, considering the number of times I thumbed my nose at security and figuratively jumped the gate to get in for free. Now, I am supposed to play the role of the nemesis I was trying to avoid. And while Chet found his niche on the visitor's side of the game, my job was all about being with the home team. Even our uniforms were different. He wore dress blues and mine consisted of black pants, a black bomber jacket, a black tie, and a black baseball cap. I looked like law enforcement and even had the badge to go with it. And I worked it. Over the course of the years, I became in charge of the media deck, the parking lots, the player's parking, and field security and had somewhere between fifteen and twenty men answering to me.

Chet may have been anointed "The Mayor of Bears Alley"—and rightfully so. But I was determined to keep the Ballard name just as lofty by showing myself to be one of the Bears top cops!

--Tom

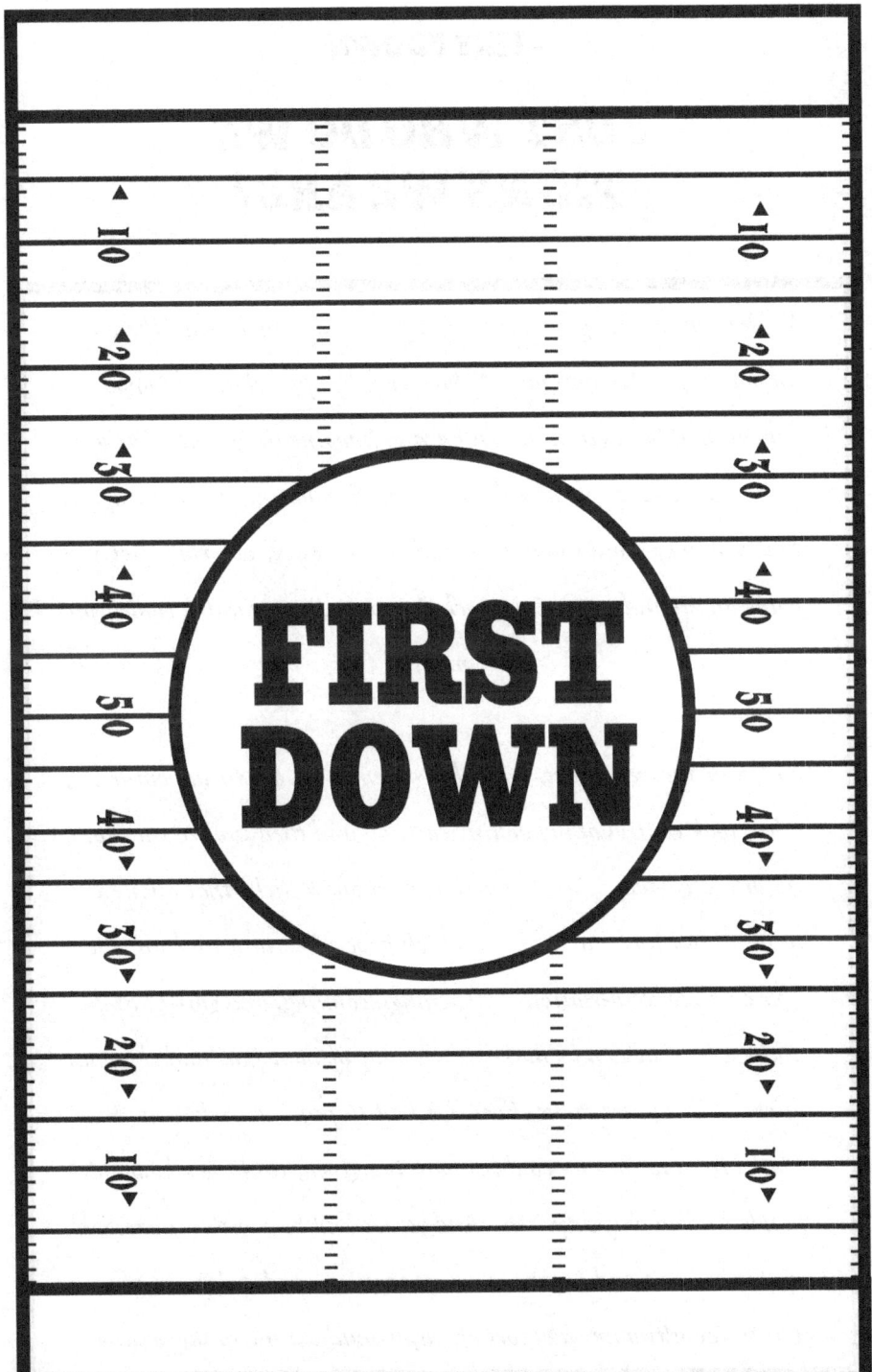

- FIRST DOWN -
JUST WHO DO WE THINK WE ARE?

We seemed to have gotten here by a fluke. We know that. There was no master plan on our part. While we fully appreciated the opportunity we had been given, it was hard to imagine the gravity. We were kids, more or less, playing dress up and thrown into the big leagues. Smart money would say we should just sit back, observe what was going on around us, and not rock the boat. But we didn't come from money.

So, from the very start, everything seemed to be an adventure. I, Chet, took control of my destiny early on and then invited me, Tom, in with a golden ticket. We both carved out a niche that allowed us to stand out and stand above which gave us certain and unbelievable access to conversations, happenings, comings, and goings; people, and events that would make us the envy of most fans and the toast of cocktail conversations. Even we had to pinch ourselves at times. Placed in situations we couldn't have imagined, rubbing elbows with people we had only admired. And yet we had been given the responsibility to serve and protect—not in that law-and-order sort of way, but in the ultimate valet sort of way. Could we rise to the occasion?

"DA BEARS" ...THE JOKE WAS FUNNY ...THE COMEDIANS, NOT SO MUCH!

It wasn't just any game. It was the NFC Playoff. The year was 1991. Like with many of these sorts of prestige games, entertainment at halftime called for big names. And in Chicago, two who were riding high at the time were funnymen actors Chris Farley and George Wendt who put the term "Da Bears" into the national vernacular with their ongoing "Saturday Night Live" spoof of overweight, over-eating, over-drinking, over-indulgent Bears' fans who pronounced the Bears, "Da Bears." Their on-camera gluttony produced spontaneous heart attacks as they extolled the superpower-winning prowess of their fan-favorite team, "Da Bears." Those skits are now part of comedy legend and the "Da Bears" has stuck.

It was just a matter of time before "Da Bears" and the Bears would collide, and needless to say, the Ballard brothers would be there to "bear" witness.

This game happened to be between the Bears and the Dallas Cowboys. There was a long rivalry between the two teams and between that tidbit this being a playoff game, it promised to be one of the most high-profile, most-watched games of the season. Let's face it which team didn't want to win against Dallas' Coach Jimmy Johnson—a man who during his tenure led Dallas to two consecutive Superbowl wins, XXVII and XXVIII.

Quarterback Troy Aikman was on the injured list and would not be playing in the game but was there to give support to the team. As things turned out, Wendt, whom most people knew as the iconic character of Norm on the hit sitcom "Cheers", was a big fan of Aikman and was determined to meet him after the game.

Because Farley and Wendt were on the field during halftime for some show antics, they were allocated a sort of all-access pass to the field. But Wendt had gone one step further. Working through the P.R. reps, he had been given an officials' pass which gave you carte blanche to go anywhere. Or so you would think. Farley didn't need that, not when you are a nationally recognized celebrity.

The game, as promised, was great…well not for "Da Bears" as much. The Cowboys took the playoff and as they made their way off the field and through Bears Alley, Wendt had somehow buried himself within the melee and was shuffled right up and through to the players' locker room, walking in with his new pal, Troy Aikman—by the way, forgetting his old pal Chris Farley who wasn't able to throw his substantial weight around in much the same way.

When the dust settled, Farley found himself without credentials, the door closed in front of him, and facing a sign which in essence read that no visitors are allowed into the locker room under any circumstances. It might as well have also read: EVEN BIG HOLLYWOOD NAMES.

Chris didn't seem to care or even tweak to the notion that he had been abandoned by Wendt and, in his "happy" state, didn't seem to know where he really was. But after a few minutes of joking and chatting, Farley did finally decide enough was enough and he wanted to go into the locker room. Despite the ominous signage, the guard who was working the door fell for Farley's blurred personality and simply opened the door and let him in.

We all know that sound, the crack when you pop open a beer. Well, that sound may as well have been a gunshot for the shitstorm it caused. Farley, already of questionable sobriety, had been standing off to the side, remarkably out of trouble, looking like an unwanted guest at a party he'd never been invited to when out of nowhere he pulls out a beer and cracks it open. One of the equipment men who happens to hear the fateful crack also doesn't have a clue who Chris Farley is and presumes he is a drunk who has stumbled in with the crowd.

Farley is quickly approached with a disingenuous, "What the fuck are you doing?" He is grabbed by the collar and starts to be escorted to the door. Farley doesn't put up a fight. But once out the door, it was asked, "Who is this guy?" Clarity didn't mean clearance and once known, he wasn't allowed back in. Farley was left standing by the door waiting for Wendt.

--Tom

By the time I was alone with Farley, he seemed to be more than a little messed up. The charm of having met a celebrity had worn off. The party was still going on inside the locker room and nothing was happening standing outside in an empty Bears Alley. Everyone had dissipated and Farley and I were just standing there.

It was sort of a sad sight, the school kid on the sidelines not having been picked for the team. He took to rocking back and forth, somewhat in a world of his own. Then comes the frenzy.

"I gotta piss," he blurts out. "I gotta piss!"

He starts hitting his back against the cement wall.

"I gotta piss. I gotta piss."

The mantra isn't lost on me but where to take him is. He's been thrown out of the Cowboy's locker room and, frankly, there is no other place close by that he has clearance to enter.

I thought for a second and it came to me. The refs had already gone for the day and their locker room should be empty. I could move Farley in and out of there without drawing attention.

As you would assume, the locker room is set up in a rather open plan. The urinals are against the wall obviously, but I am able to sit on the centrally located bench and not lose sight of Farley who, in his condition, was not a wise thing to do.

He does what comes naturally and after, as he is finishing up and zipping up his zipper, I take the opportunity to steal one of the lines from the "Saturday Night Live" sketch.

"Hey Todd! How many heart attacks have you had today?" I ask, breaking what had been a long time of no conversation. What did I have to lose, reaching out to him with this non-sensical throwback reference?

Without missing a beat and clearly shaking off the fog he'd been in, he falls completely into his fan character. He approaches me and hoists his leg onto the bench. "About half a dozen," he answers with that unmistakable over-enunciated accent as if I was sitting around the set table. How many heart attacks do you think I had?

He thanked me for appreciating the SNL skit and for getting him to the restroom in time and we walked out and waited for Wendt—who not long after emerged, whisked Farley along and both disappeared out. We never really spoke after the SNL reference but that was enough.

I always had a suspicion "Da Bears" would make its way into our lives somehow. It was just too big of a cultural phenomenon to let go of.

I just never thought it would be alone with one of the stars whom I had just escorted to a mercy piss in a restricted area. Would I have done that for just anybody?

Over the years, I came across plenty of "stars" who intermittently put me in my place, kept me in my place, showed me my place, reminded me of my place, or took me to a higher place. But even all these years later, I look back at Chris Farley and remember fondly that whether I play the role of Frain or fan, I will always be proud to have just been one of "Da Bears!"

--Chet

CHICAGO: THERE'S JUST SOMETHING ABOUT CHICAGO!

You can't just show up in Chicago, play against the Bears and not have a sense of history or a sense of sentimentality wash over you. Fun fact: the Bears have the most retired player numbers in the entire NFL. Why is that? Because the Bears have been a football organization from the start of football…family-owned and family-run…and make up a beloved patch in the quilting of Chicago's social blanket—as an entrenched symbol of the city as recognizable and iconic as jazz, deep dish pizza, the mob, Lake Shore Drive along the Magnificent Mile, Lake Michigan, the devoted blue-collar fan Johnny Lunch Bucket, and of course Soldier Field. It is why the elders of the league pay respect when coming to the shrine of a stadium and understand that a game may just be a game…but the Bears are an experience.

Except for the grass! As the saying goes: "The grass is always greener on the other side of the fence." Well, the grass may have been green at old Soldier Field, but it was no surface anyone really wanted to play on. Players, coaches, and teams, in general, may have been sentimental about playing in Chicago and against the Bears, but, it seems, no one was particularly fond of playing on the turf of old Soldier Field.

If you don't believe me, you can believe the NFL which would conduct its own surveys of playing conditions and player satisfaction within the stadiums, all the stadiums. And, yes, old Soldier Field would rate at the bottom of the rankings for natural turf fields.

Why?

Soldier Field is not owned by a corporation or a private entity. It is owned by the City of Chicago and therefore maintained by the park district. To that end, the city maintained the property. But to say they didn't give a shit about what the needs of the players on the field were, in terms of an uneven playing field—yes, there were divots and potholes for players to contend with along with bumps from mud, or rocks embedded within the underlying soil, and soil so packed down that hitting the ground was like hitting cement—was a colossal understatement. They were city employees—hired to strictly maintain, not to curate.

The ironic part was that I had another job selling lawn products at that time. While I tried to talk to the field manager, Ken Mrock, about improving the conditions at Soldier Field, it would have taken a city contract, which was simply a no-go. But part of my job was to go off to Lambeau Field a couple of times a week, selling them fertilizers and various products to keep their field pristine. Then on Sundays, I would show back up at Soldier Field to watch player after player trip and get hurt on the field of dreams...not the field that was a dream.

Yes, it is true, the grass is greener. But it was greener over at Lambeau. I saw to that. Sentimentality aside, Soldier Field may have put on a good show for those visitors who couldn't get enough of all things Chicago. But for those of us in the know. There is a difference between a good show...and a shit show.

--Chet

Los Angeles has its celebrities. New York has its pretensions. In Chicago, we have our sports—from hockey to baseball to basketball to, of course, the Bears. It is easy to take that for granted because it is just part of the fabric of the city. Sometimes it takes the acknowledgment of an outsider to point out just how good we have it. But I hardly expected a compliment from Jon Gruden.

Jon Gruden was as about as hard-nosed a coach as there was. A 15-year coaching veteran with the Oakland Raiders, then took the Tampa Bay Buccaneers to a Super Bowl victory (achieving the personal note of being the then youngest head coach at the time to ever win a Super Bowl at 39 years old), and then back to the Raiders until his "resignation" after personal racist and homophobic emails surfaced. Along the way, he picked up the nickname "Chucky" for his close resemblance to the doll of slasher movie fame and his stoic resting facial expression. While coaching, he was a personality to contend with—take no prisoners with the players and was quick with the sarcastic one-liners with the media. And that is why he loved Chicago.

He thought, like him, we had grit. Chicagoans work hard to earn the right to play hard. He liked that, about all our hometown teams, not just the Bears. I know this because he told me this.

It was during the period of his career when he had turned to broadcast. After he left Tampa Bay and before being asked to return to Oakland, Gruden did a several-year stint along with Al Michaels doing play-by-play and color commentary for the networks. After one pre-game media meeting, he emerged with Al Michaels and I asked if they needed an escort to the broadcast booth, which they accepted.

While on our way, out of the clear blue, Gruden turned to me and said, "I like Chicago. This is a good sports town…". He rattled off the teams and what he liked about them. "You've had a good year," he punctuated. I couldn't help but have a sense of pride as he spoke.

It seems the sportscasters were in lockstep when it comes to Chicago. Chris Collinsworth enjoyed the town, John Madden also took note of the grit of the town and the team, and Al Michaels loved coming to Chicago to cover the Bears. But Michaels' love affair with the city was about having an affair. He's been cheating on us, the Bears, with the Blackhawks. You see, Michaels, unknown to most, is a huge hockey fan and when in town tries to make a Blackhawks game, time and schedule permitting. Don't worry Al, your secret's safe with us.

But there is just something about Chicago…and moreover, the Bears. We get that a lot, mostly from the average people who work the games. The equipment managers from visiting teams for instance notice a difference when they come to Chicago. Perhaps it is something in the air. Perhaps it is a vibe we send out—something unspoken but registers loud and clear. Even the hard-nosed Gruden couldn't help but notice. We are Chicago. We are sports….and good sports at that.

--Tom

When it came to sentimentality, one visitor stands out: Jerry Glanville. He stands out for a number of reasons.

First, it is hard to get past his appearance. He is a caricature of the cowboy that he actually wasn't—wearing a long black duster, cowboy hat, and boots—his look was an affectation left over from his days as a coach for the Houston Oilers.

Then it was his demeanor. Quirky…okay. He is notable, or more appropriately notorious, for a couple of things. As a big fan of Elvis Presley, he always left two tickets for every game at the Will Call window for Elvis—just in case. Second, he coined the now famous, nee 'infamous' phrase "N-F-L…which stands for 'not for long'." And lastly, he had a penchant for driving cars that were replicas of cars driven by the late actor James Dean. He was a character for sure, earning the title.

He moved on from the Oilers to the Atlanta Falcons in 1990 during the heady days of Deion Sanders' tenure. During that time, within the '91 season, they came to Chicago for a game. As my job specified, I waited outside the locker room for the visiting coaches to walk out and I would traditionally ask them if their needs were being met. He, on this day, walked out of the visitor's locker room alone to find me standing there, as was appropriate. He was in his long black duster and me in my uniform and he just started talking.

"This is where the Packers and the Bears had their stuff," he began like an old history buff referring to a time back in the 70's when the two teams' locker rooms were across from each other and when they met in the tunnel it caused a now legendary pre-game brawl. He seemed rather excited about the memory and standing in a place of history. I told him I could take him to the actual locker rooms if he liked.

The locker rooms had long since been converted into rows with sealed lockers. Back in the day, they would have had open-facing lockers as opposed to today's with doors and locks. But the room itself had the same layout as all those years ago and the same showers. The rooms were free at the time, so there was no problem with us walking in.

Once inside, he was transfixed as if he had never seen a locker room before. He walked around, looked around, and gathered it all in. We did the same for the home team locker room and he just nodded as he looked around. Didn't speak. Just took it all in. Had he come to church? We did the same for the coaches' locker rooms. By now he was getting some looks from people passing by. Who is this cowboy of a man, just staring at the obvious with such intent?

Once he had his fill, we went back out into the tunnel and looked out on the field and he finally spoke. "This is what football is all about," he muttered. "This is what the NFL is all about. And you can see it in the runway out. It is just the vibe. The aura. It is like the spirits from the old days are all here."

Again, he was taking it in and wondering how he could express what he was feeling to his players. How could this be a motivating moment? I tell you, just by watching him, I couldn't help but feel the history he was grabbing at. It was infectious.

He was old school…or at least believed in the old school. He spoke about not liking the new attitude of players with their multi-million-dollar contracts and how they didn't mesh with the kind of 'street fighter' mentality of the older players who still occupied a place of honor on the field beside them. The battle is now within the team and not completely against the other team…at least psychologically. He lamented the fact that these days you have to go through metal detectors to get to locker rooms.

Bottom line, he longed for what he saw in Soldier Field—history still being lived.

And I was proud that the Ballard boys were still witnessing it... still living it.

--Tom

Old Soldier Field was not only a place of history and a place of tradition but was also the location for a once-a-year national phenomenon known as the College All-Star Game. It had come to an end long before my tenure began but believe me, when I tell you, it was the talk of many a visiting coach who thought back fondly on the game and the times.

The tradition lasted from 1934 through 1976 and the concept was simple: the all-stars of college teams played a one-time-only yearly game against the all-stars of the NFL. It was all for charity. It was all for fun. And don't think for a minute the college players were outgunned. On more than one occasion they came out victorious.

Why did it mean so much to all these visiting coaches? Well, a lot of the old-time coaches in the NFL got their start in college football. There was a sentimentality to and for the college players. Not to mention, the game being played in the stately Soldier Field only added to the prestige.

With a game so popular, so long entrenched, you might think it would be a tradition that would have lasted in perpetuity. But good sense and business sense got the better of longevity and sentimentality. These were assets in the making, these college players and it eventually occurred to someone in high places that these potentially high-numbered

NFL draft picks were being placed in a precarious situation. They were the best the season had to offer. Why risk injury from what the NFL's best had to offer? The kibosh was inevitable. But the memories live on.

To this day, I can't shake how fondly visitors looked back on that once-a-year game. But moreover, they considered it part of the many valued moments that make up Soldier Field, the Bears, and greater Chicago. The visitors would look at me as if I had something to do with those events by simply being a part of the Soldier Field community—even though the College All-Star game had long since been a thing of the past. Time and time again, I was gladly reminded to respect where I stood and what it stood for because it just reminds me…us, actually, my brother and I… that history's moments are fluid. And because of our positions and proximity, it was ours to drink up.

--Chet

I DIDN'T SIGN UP FOR THIS... OR DID I?

Yes, we had our functions. We had our assignments. We had our tasks. But perhaps I (Chet) with my "Chief" hat and Mayoral influence, and I (Tom) with my badge and swagger were perceived as to be in more elevated positions than we really were. To have more power. To be able to get more solved. But we weren't. Most times that perception just got us what we wanted. But on rare occasions, it put us in awkward positions that, had they played out the way they were predicted to do so, we may have been the wrong people for the job at hand.

Don't get us wrong. We took our jobs seriously and the responsibilities that went with them. But some things are just above our pay grade.

Mike Ditka. Those two words, that name, can raise cheers and jeers depending on whom you ask in Chicago. And boy, did he milk the attention. The slicked-back hair, brittle mustache, chomping on a cigar, neatly attired; was he a mob boss or a football coach? He had the disposition of a bulldog and the gamesmanship of a punk. And that is what got the job done.

He was Chicago's guy when he took the Bears to the Super Bowl in '85. In fact, over the course of his career, he was one of only two coaches to be carried off the field from a game win in triumph by his team members. Moreover, he became the face of football, a national treasure. As much as he treated the media like second-class citizens—making anyone who asked a perceptively stupid question look like the fool they were meant to be—he loved all that media gave him. He was Johnny Lunch Bucket from the blue-collar steel country of Pennsylvania who was now appearing on "Saturday Night Live," had a lucrative string of endorsements, and even an eponymous restaurant chain. When you thought of the Bears back in the glory years, you thought of Ditka. When you thought of football in general back then, you thought of Mike Ditka.

So, after eleven high-profile seasons, why let a good man go?

The official statement from a teary-eyed Michael McCaskey, the president of the Bears organization—who despite being the boss, was less respected than ousted Ditka—was to seek "fresh ideas." The real reason people were stating, was that Ditka had all become too much of being about Ditka. The sideline temper tantrums, the larger-than-life personality, the outside business dealings, and the "never wrong" mentality had all become too much of a good thing gone bad. Although Ditka held his head high on the day of the announcement, Chicagoans were shocked at the blindside play. Love him or hate him, Ditka was their guy.

Until he wasn't.

It came to pass that the sheen on Ditka may have been a bit of a tarnish. Once gone, he was easier to see in hindsight rather than still in your face. He had burned a lot of bridges just being…well…Ditka. The bravado rankled more than a few fans and colleagues alike. His cashing in on his clout, in retrospect, seemed unseemly. His treatment and mistreatment of players and the media, as well as his general disrespect for authority left people with a bad taste regarding his bad taste. As a result, Ditka did what no one expected—stepped away from coaching…choosing, of course, to color commentate for television.

Whether it was ego…oh hell, who are we kidding…of course ego played into his coming back to coaching. By 1997, he was ready to take his rightful place along the sidelines once again. This time with the New Orleans Saints. And it was just a matter of time before the Saints and the Bears were set to clash. After missing for nearly half a decade, Ditka was back at Soldier Field but on the wrong side of the grass.

It was my job to greet the visiting players, the coaches…the teams in their entirety…at the gate where the buses would drop them from the hotel. It was October 5th, and there was a buzz in the air that "the coach" was coming back. The buses arrived at the North Gate, which just so happened to be accessible to fans. On this day, with the imminent arrival of Ditka, there were hundreds of people waiting—enough so, that we had to set up bike racks to keep the people back. We waited for a worst-case scenario to unfold but everyone arrived without incident. Still, when Ditka got to the locker room, the media was at a frenzied pitch. He was in his glory. Now more Christian than combative, he may as well have been the prodigal son returning.

After the formalities were over, Ditka emerged from the locker room, no longer in his trademark sweater and tie but rather in a black leather bomber jacket. Always the tough guy. He lit up one of his monstrous cigars and turned to the smattering of cameras around him. It was somewhat chaotic, and he seemed to thrive on that. I stepped up in the midst of the confusion and offered myself to Ditka, stating something to the effect that I could be available should he feel uncomfortable or in need of being escorted safely to wherever he may need to go.

He looked at me with all that Ditka bravado and uttered, "Whadda ya think…somebody's gonna try to kill me?"

Until that moment, I hadn't thought of that. It was a good line for the few media standing around to pick up on. But on second thought, in the abstract anything could happen. The prevailing feeling was that Ditka cashed in when times were good here and left the team in shambles on the way out. So, yeah, being back in hostile territory, there were plenty of rabid fans out there. The question I had, now that he brought it up, was:

had he ever been threatened before this? Did he really think someone may take their shot? And shouldn't we have planned for this?

It was certainly above my pay grade to take a bullet. Way above my pay grade. But it did get me thinking about the overall vulnerability of players, coaches, and high-level V.I.Ps. And while I may have had the title of "security", I suddenly felt very insecure.

"I don't need you," Ditka huffed my way and walked away.

Ditka went on with the day, incident free, but I couldn't get past the notion that it was me who dodged the bullet.

--Tom

George Mandich, the head of NFL security, would have almost been comical if he wasn't so serious. Each time he approached me, he appeared to be the very caricature of what a former FBI man would look like. The ever-present trench coat certainly did him no favors in terms of lightening his look. As such, it was hard not to give him respect for his position because he, and rightfully so, took things so seriously.

I figured this would be just another ordinary game day. As ordinary as it gets when the Green Bay Packers play the Chicago Bears. This was very early on in my years and so as a teenager of about 17 years old, I was simply looking forward to seeing the game. That was until Mandich approached me.

"We need to be on heightened alert, taking an extra lookout during the game," he declares.

"Okay," I assure him. "But what is going on?"

"There is a death threat out for James Lofton."

Lofton was a high-profile player, one of the leading receivers on the Packer's lineup. The NFL had gotten an alert that there was going to potentially be a hit taken out on Lofton while he was at Soldier Field—something about retribution for bad gambling debts, the details of which were never shared—and, by the sounds of things, 17-year-old Chet Ballard would be one of the fine folks assigned to stop it. Wait! What?

You didn't joke with George, and this was no laughing matter. But really? When and how did I become deputized into Lofton's secret service?

"We just all need to be on point and be looking out for anything suspicious."

What did I know from "suspicious" at my age and real-life experiences? If you are wondering what the plan of action was, so was I. There was none. All I knew was that when Lofton was going out on the field for the pre-game warm-up, I was to shadow him. Why me? Definitely bad timing, when Lofton came out of the locker room and I happened to be the only one standing there.

"Do you want me to walk you out?" I asked.

"Yeah, yeah," he quickly answered.

There were a number of fans in the bleachers and some Paparazzi shooting the only shots I wanted to know about that day, camera shots, as Lofton went out on the field. I can say I was too naïve to think that this threat was anything but a threat. Still, that didn't stop my adrenalin levels from peaking. Just who did he piss off enough to make a death threat? The mob? I mean, what if? Was I really supposed to take a bullet for this guy? I was pretty sure there was nothing about that in the Andy Frain hiring papers.

The game was ruined for me. I couldn't concentrate on the action on the field when at any given moment there could be action coming from anywhere. In my mind's eye, I never could believe that there would be an actual assassination right there at Soldier field but apparently, others did. By games' end when nothing had occurred, Lofton was escorted discreetly out of one of the less conspicuous doors, ushered out of the Stadium, and presumably left to his own devices from there on. There was a collective sigh of relief.

I know I should look back on this moment with pride, that I was the one picked to guard such a valued asset. They would only rely on the most trusted employee for such a privileged situation. Right?

Not so much. I was standing in the wrong place at the wrong time. I had no training in security, was never on the wrong end of a gun, and never in front of someone willing to use one. What good was I really going to be? Because in the end, no one ever told me what I was supposed to do if the threat was real, the would-be killer emerged, and I was the "lucky" one there to confront him.

From this, there are two things I know for sure:

One, James Lofton needs a better poker face.

Two, I need to read the fine print in the job description section.

Really, George Mandich—former FBI and head of all NFL security in Chicago—was I the best you could come up with? What did you expect me to do?

--Chet

Ditka may have been all mouth and the line about being killed may have been his idea of a media soundbite meant to be a joke. Security, or the lack thereof, never left my mind over the years.

The word "fan" is short for "fanatic" and that is exactly what they can be. So, it stuck in my mind that, while we assume the "fans" will be on their best behavior, who could really tell who's out there? I think back to the time when the tennis player Monica Seles was stabbed in the shoulder blade right on the court at Wimbledon in 1993 by a crazed fan.

So, it shouldn't have shocked me in 2001 when the Bears were matched against the Tampa Bay Buccaneers, and another mouthy member of their team, Keyshawn Johnson didn't receive the warmest reception from one of Chicago's "fanatics."

Keyshawn Johnson was all "that" at USC when he was a star college player. Perhaps it was there where he began to believe his own publicity. As an early draft pick for the New York Jets, his reputation as an outstanding wide receiver was only superseded by his big hot head. Yes, he was one of those players—who constantly, it seemed, looked for conflict…and found it.

That kind of bravado can be what makes a killer player just that: a killer. But it does nothing for gamesmanship and team building. By the time he signed his multi-million-dollar contract with Tampa Bay as one of the bright hopes for the flailing team, his reputation was sealed. Yes, as I said, he believed he was all that.

Tampa Bay beat us on the day of our match. And I, along with some of my guys, was standing in the Bears' Alley positioned just under the overhang waiting for the players to come off the field. As Keyshawn made his way towards us, someone from above poured a full beer onto Johnson's head, soaking him. It was a direct hit for which he didn't flinch, didn't look up, just kept walking.

As the guys scrambled to get a look to see who may have done the deed, I approached the non-plussed Johnson. The hot head got a cool soaking and was surprisingly calm. I expected outrage or for him to be at least enraged. But no.

I began a profuse but empty apology on behalf of the Bears organization, Chicagoans in general, and the city at large. I couldn't believe what I had seen…and on my watch no less. His reaction had me more stunned than the actual event.

"Don't worry about it," he muttered. "It happens to me all the time. At all the stadiums."

Instantly, I flipped the switch from there-must-have-been-something-we-could-have-done to pointing the blame squarely where it belonged—at Keyshawn Johnson, whose mouth and manner got him into this situation on a regular basis. I quickly realized you simply can't protect people…from themselves. And with that, all was secure at Soldier Field.

--Tom

JUST BETWEEN US GUYS...

You just never know when you are standing there and bullshit is being flown or a piece of honest insight, retrospection, or introspection is being shared. That was the thrill of the periphery—you never knew what you were going to get! Mostly, it was just the guys shooting the shit. On several occasions, if you listened closely, and we did, you came home with a story that stuck with you because it gave perspective on how the guys played the game despite how they felt about those with whom they were playing. The following is just one from each of us that stuck.

We were playing the Washington Redskins, as they were called back then when political correctness wasn't part of the name game in football. Steve Spurrier was the coach…and boy did he know football…college football, that is. Yes, I said college football.

Spurrier was in the College Football Hall of Fame—having achieved his coaching prowess on the fields of the likes of Georgia Tech, the Tampa Bay Bandits, South Carolina, and Duke. He won close to a dozen college bowls and was a five-time coach of the year. He was, for the lack of a better term, a legend on the college level…which even dates back to being the Heisman Trophy winner as a college quarterback for the University of Florida during his early playing days. He went on to play for the NFL for a decade or so before coaching at the college level. The natural progression was to coach for the NFL.

The Redskins were lucky to have him. He joined in the early 2000s; the team was nothing to write home about then. Spurrier was brought in to "turn things around"—as new coaches are expected to do.

The game on this day was not a playoff game but should the Redskins win, they would have had a chance to be heading to the playoffs. So, there was a lot on the line for the Redskins. Spurrier seemed to know it… but did the team?

As it turned out, the Redskins lost.

As was my normal position, I was waiting outside the locker room when Spurrier walked out after the game. Normally, he was an affable kind of guy. Not today. The loss seemed to hit him hard.

As I approached to see if he needed anything, he took notice of several players walking ahead of him. They were joking and laughing and didn't seem to care that they had just lost an important game which effectively put them out of the season's running. Spurrier paused and stared for a moment and his face said it all. Disbelief. He then turned to me.

"See those guys right there?" he began, pointing to the players. "Does it look like they just lost one of the season's most important games? For them?"

I wasn't sure what to say. Clearly, he wanted to both vent and make a point and I was the sympathetic ear nearby.

"Not really," was the best I could come up with.

"This is the problem with the NFL," he continued. "On the college level, I can pick the players that I want. I could recruit the quarterbacks and work with them. I could pick who I wanted to play with. But this is the NFL where the owners and the personnel guys make those decisions and this (pointing again to the jokesters in front of him) is who I get. I have to work with who I've got. And if they are not all on the same page, this is what happens."

There wasn't anything for me to say. And I don't think he was looking for me to say anything. He just needed to vent his clear and present frustration. I simply nodded my understanding and that was enough. I wasn't sure if this was the epiphany moment that put him over the edge. But at the end of that season, Spurrier quit. He admitted at the time that he was lured to the NFL by the money and that perhaps the Redskins were not the best fit into which to have made that leap. He went with the team that offered the most money and not the best situation.

I think back on that moment outside the locker room when a prideful man had to accept defeat—not on the field but in his career. It changed the way I look at each team as they enter the game and leave the game. Are they a brotherhood of men or a collection of players? Because that will forecast the outcome of the game more times than not. I can now determine when the team arrives when they step off the bus if they are a cohesive band of brothers and whether they will have a good game or not. I have seen first-hand the difference between a gathering of really great players who can't win a game and, on the other hand, lesser talent who collectively make up a bonded brotherhood that sweeps the field on a given Sunday.

When Spurrier got on that bus to leave that day, angry and defeated on several levels, I knew he was gone for good. I had been brought into his confidence. I could read between the lines. He wouldn't be their coach for much longer, but he would be mine for the rest of my career. Because as little impact as he thought he had in the NFL, he had a great impact on me. I could now read the room and was left with an insight into the game I probably never would have worked out just by day-to-day comings and goings. Given that, I will always thank Coach Spurrier…not the team coach, but the life coach.

--Tom

As an employee of Andy Frain, one of the stipulations was that you didn't wear your uniform out on the streets. Therefore, we were to wear our 'civies' to and from Soldier Field and change into our uniforms once there. For that process, there was a designated Andy Frain locker room. Fine. At least for the others. Not for me. Not for the "Mayor of Bears Alley." I may have started out in the Andy Frain locker room, but it wasn't long before I and an equipment manager pal commandeered a spot in the ref's locker room for our personal use. Of course, it was wrong… but no one questioned the "Mayor."

While getting ready one Sunday, my buddy lets me know that Jim McMahon has arrived. Although he was still actively playing with the NFL—he was most notably with the Bears during the Superbowl season but had subsequently skipped to six different teams over the course of his career—McMahon was here on this day as a visitor but wanted no one to know that he was at the stadium. That would be easier said than done but certainly a job for the "Mayor."

The refs had gone on to start their routine of pre-game meetings and so sneaking him into the locker room was easy enough. What to do with him from there was going to take some thought.

McMahon was as colorful a character as you got at the time in football. Known for both on and off-field antics, he was once fined for wearing a headband with an unauthorized Adidas logo on it during a game. And he sported an attitude, that often got him at odds with the Bears owner Mike McCaskey and Coach Mike Ditka.

Just saying the name of Ditka got him going. Inevitably, Ditka's name came up in conversation. We stood there as he spouted, spewed, and spit everything that came to mind—none of it flattering, none of it complimentary, none of it repeatable. I can say it punctuated with the lingering line: "I hate that piece of shit!"

Those kinds of outbursts are never good as they can be leaked to the press for instance. McMahon didn't strike me as a player or a man who gave a damn about what people thought about him or his thoughts about you. Dangerous and volatile are not a winning combination for good gamesmanship. Then again, the colorful and bombastic Mike Ditka didn't always bring out the best in others.

At that point, I realized my role in this and other moments like this was cemented. Jim McMahon needed the "Mayor." I was the fresh meat in the room. The fresh audience. I provided a new set of ears to listen to what were probably tired rantings by now.

I accepted the role gladly. Sure, it gave me a story to share over a beer with the guys. Moreover, it provided insight I found interesting about player and team dynamics. At what point does the team showman have to be a show-off? To what end? From my perspective, it only causes fracture not bonding.

Over the course of his career, McMahon was plagued with injuries—from a well-publicized shoulder incident with the Bears to concussions too many to mention over the years. But what about the league's most dangerous injury—that of the bruised ego? It can ruin a reputation or take down a career just as easily. I was trying to determine, there in the locker room, whether McMahon had a bruised ego or was trying to cause one.

Nevertheless, the bruised ego is the cancer no one talks about within the NFL as a legitimate by-product of success run amok. What had Ditka done to McMahon to warrant such an outburst? What was wrong with McMahon that he felt the need to invalidate others who elevated him to the levels of success he'd achieved? And I was playing my role in it all, the cancer host. The spreader. The listener. Giving credence by simply being there.

I walked away from that moment no longer sure if I was just the "Mayor". Or am I now an armchair psychologist…or worse yet an ego oncologist. One thing for sure, when I put on my Andy Frain hat—remember, I had custom-made mine with the word "Chief" embroidered across the front—I know now, I am wearing many hats.

--Chet

SILENCE IS GOLDEN... AT LEAST THE GOLDEN RULE!

There is nothing like the sound of the crush from a tackle as heard from the sidelines. It is chilling. That bone-crushing thud is as much a part of the game as the call of the "hike" and the roar of the crowd. The experience of football is as much audible as it is visual, which is why during the Covid days of empty stadiums, broadcasters edited in the sounds of cheering bleacher fans so as to not lose the ambiance of the moment. It would seem that no one has a tougher job to paint the picture of the excitement of the game both visually and audibly than the journalists whose very job it is to telegraph, in their medium, the action of the game. How do you write about noise?

Well, that is exactly the crux of this moment. Noise...and the price to be paid for making it.

So, the last place you would expect silence…and I am talking library-level silence…is the press box at the stadium. But it is there, in this most sacred of denizens where creativity flourishes that noise goes to die. Do not expect cheers. No jeers. No shouts of excitement, sideline coaching, and quarterbacking, play predictions, or rooting for the favorite or the underdog. No outbursts of any kind. And that included me.

I got my taste of the press box atmosphere early on when I used to sneak into the games. The press box was my hiding spot. Hiding in plain sight. Back then, in old Soldier Field, the press box, like all the boxes at the time, from the owner's boxes right on down to the coaches' boxes, was far from glamorous. It had windows you could swing open, and a two-tiered seating system along long tables with barstool seats. Everyone—the fifty or so journalists, from local to national—was assigned a spot, with the more prominent publications getting the more central seating. There was certainly a class and caste system in the place but there was also a brotherhood among the men.

Back in those older days, there was noise—the noise of productivity. Typewriters. Journalists were on deadlines and had to file stories by the end of the game and the cacophony of typewriter keys was ever-present as game highlights were turned into print adventures.

By the time, the press box was established within the new Soldier Field things were even quieter. Computers were the norm, people had more space in which to work as the box now stretched the length of the distance between the two thirty-yard lines on the field, and there were assistants within the box to cater to your needs allowing for less of the journalists to move around. It was much more of a modern newsroom than the old rickety press box.

The one thing that did carry over from the old press box to this new "newsroom" was the absolute rule of silence. And I was to see first-hand what happens when you break the rules.

It was 2003, the first year in the new facility, and the Bears were considered a team to keep your eye on. They had talent. They were competitive. The press room was filled each week covering the Bears and whomever they were playing against. And that meant journalists from visiting teams were also present. Despite that fact, no one dared showed their colors, played partisan patriot, or in any way declared favoritism for one team over the other. Chicago is an emotional city. In a close game especially, it is hard to keep your opinions to yourself. But the press room was considered Switzerland—a neutral territory in the war zone. And while "silence" was presumably a gentleman's agreement at every stadium, not everyone got the memo at Soldier Field.

What was I doing up there on this fateful day? Well, I worked in radio sales as a day job, and for this particular game, one of my radio cronies who worked for the communications side of the NFL happened to be at the game. Between assignments, I snuck up to the press box to check on my buddy and watch part of the game.

It was a close one and at this moment, the call was fourth and one with the visitors in control of the ball. We all love a good nail-biting moment. Some apparently more than others. As the play commenced, with the ball in motion, one visiting print journalist leaped to his feet and screamed out loud "Yeah!" in support of the now winning first down. It was the shot heard around the world…well, at least heard around the room. The other journalists went ballistic, demanding that he sit down and shut up. The now chastised journalist threw his arms up in defeat, knowing he let the moment get the best of him and he had done wrong. He sat down in journalistic disgrace.

That should have been the end of it. But no. One other clearly flustered journalist in the room formally complained about the antics and security was called into action. Now, I may have the badge, but the press box was not my beat. They had their own security team in place. I just stood back and watched as a guard approached the confused visitor, explaining to him that his actions were not to be tolerated and that he would have to leave. With that, he was escorted from the room.

To add insult to injury, as he left, the others stood and cheered… collectively breaking the very rule for which he was being ousted. Tough crowd.

I didn't spend any more time in the box that day and certainly minded myself during subsequent visits. I could be prone to letting my emotions get the better of me and quite frankly didn't want to be on the receiving end of the keyboard clicker's outrage after a misdirected outburst. As I said, Chicago can be an emotional town, and never more so than at the game.

In this press box, it may be said that hell hath no fury like the power of the press… or at least those in control of it…where the written word will get you a Pulitzer Prize, and the spoken word will get you the boot! "YEAH!"

So, I will leave you with one final word: "Shhhhh….!"

--Tom

THOSE WERE THE DAYS... WE HAVE THE MEMORIES... THEY HAVE NO RESPECT!

"Who are all those old fuckers," one of the young buck players carelessly asked his fellow teammates too loud to take back as he passed the legends standing in Bears Alley. It was loud enough for me to hear and presumably loud enough for those to whom he was referring to hear as well. It was not like he was a prestige player, just rank and file. They were dignitaries. Game icons who were asked back to be honored before the game and recognized for the groundbreakers they were. But that, of course, was lost on the young pissant who could only see his God-given gifts as nothing more than entitlement and not having been paved for him by the very people whose reputations he just pissed all over.

One of those people was Elmer Angsman…the Elmer Angsman… who practically goes back as far as football itself. Considered one of the four horsemen of Notre Dame playing on the 1943 National Championship team, he made a name for himself as a Chicago kid who made good when he was drafted by the NFL as the youngest player ever at 20 years old in 1946. It was the Cardinals he played for back when the Cardinals were still a Chicago team. He was considered one of owner Charlie Bidwell's "Dream Backfield" and was selected for the first-ever Pro Bowl. He was that Elmer Angsman!

My Uncle Fran knew Angsman. But of course, my Uncle Fran knew everyone. If we thought we had clout in Bears Alley, Uncle Fran had the clout of the town. He would meet with Angsman at yet another favorite watering hole not far from Comiskey Park, where the Cardinals would play back in the day. The Cardinals and the Bears in Angsman's day were your hometown, cross-town rivals and Angsman was full of those "those were the days" stories.

I got to meet him over lunch with Uncle Fran. Lunch was never lunch, it was an event. Even the place was a step back in time and you were simply expected to sit back and enjoy the ride. Between Angsman and Uncle Fran, I just shut my mouth and enjoyed the banter, "those days!"

I must tell you, for a man in his elder years, Elmer cut an impressive figure. He was taller than I would have thought and broad, with a football player's build still and a strong speaking voice. Usually, Uncle

Fran was the attention-getter in the room but Elmer Angsman gave him a run for the money. He regaled the table with stories of old and when he went out to Los Angeles to play and found Jayne Mansfield an opposing fan. He told us about everything from her foul mouth to his having to wash his own uniform in the locker room sink while on the road back then just to have something clean for the next game.

He talked about how they were paid a pittance back then and that all the players had to maintain "day jobs" just so they could afford to play "professional" football. So, because of having day jobs, they practiced football at night.

He was a character. A drinker. An orator. Everyone knew his name. Everyone, clearly, except for the newbies walking through Bears Alley that day who did little more than throw attitude to Elmer and the other icons of football past, standing waiting to be honored. What made the scene even more egregious is the fact that as the new players were coming off the field, the icons were holding out their hands to slap theirs in appreciation.

"Who are all those old fuckers?" was what they got in return.

Elmer had recognized and acknowledged me in the Alley from having met him with Uncle Fran during that lunch and despite the rude comment, he seemed non-plussed by the whole thing. Taking it like the gentleman that he was. Perhaps he hadn't even heard the comment amid the frenzy of the moment. I hoped that was the case.

The bile rose in my throat. I just wanted to march Elmer into the locker room, sit the guys down and say, "Listen to this man." He paved the way for these players, these players who now make more in one game than he made in a season. They have no idea just how much they are catered to, even pampered, to play the very same game that Elmer gladly washed his own clothes to be part of. Still, even if these iconic gentlemen were nobody of significance in the history of the game, they were at the very least fans and that, in its own right, deserved respect from the present-day players.

People will tell you it all comes down to money. It's not that people don't deserve their fair slice of the pie, but you should have to prove yourself before you are given more money than you need in a lifetime, in a single contract. Money has changed the man, changed the player, changed the game. I say that as the Bears bemoan the fact they didn't pick Patrick Mahomes during the draft when they had the opportunity to do so and now the half-billion-dollar star is tearing it up for the Kansas City Chiefs. Who knew he would be worth that kind of money? Is he? Isn't every player an injury away from obsolescence? That is not just my opinion. Ask Jerry Glanville and Phil Rivers. They will and have said the same.

I was talking with tight end Jim Thornton who was known on the Bears team as "Robocop" because of his huge physique—a bulldozer of a man. You could have easily thought of him as a Rob Gronkowski before there was a Rob Gronkowski. Gronk was a multi-million-dollar player in his own right while Robocop made a better-than-average living who wasn't complaining but wasn't paid on that very same level. Back in his day blocking was more important than catching, but he, like Gronk, could do both.

I was waiting for the equipment manager after a game when Thornton happened by, "Hey Tommy," he waved and just sat to chat. At the time, the national news was filled with the scandal of a player who had allegedly assaulted his girlfriend. The news had clearly bothered him. He talked about the entitlement issues of today's players and how they think they can get away with anything because they are exalted by the team or organization…even the fans, who might not know better. And the more you are paid, the more you are protected.

That conversation segued to the days when he was at his peak, the late 80s into the 90s. "You didn't compare what you were making based on what the other guy was making," he explained. "Pay inequality had a direct effect on the morale of the team." The inference was clear, they were a team and not a group of stars who happened to be playing together.

Bottom lining it, he didn't feel the game was ruined, just changed… and not for the better. Cohesion is the casualty.

I see that all the time. I can tell as the players pass me by whether they are going to win or lose…or, at the very least, whether it will be an interesting game…just by their faces. Some are in isolation with their headphones tuning out the world. Some are oblivious. Some are chatting. Some eyes forward, some diverted. But I can tell if there is that cohesion existing. Are they partners or just players, just a group with a collective goal or a solidified team? There is a difference, and that difference can make or break the game. There is an attitude.

Yes, it is a multi-billion-dollar industry, and everyone should share the wealth. But you should earn your share and respect how you earn it. Between salaries, and endorsements, production companies, entertainment opportunities, and financial investments…where is the loyalty to the game? Who has time to play the game? Is the hustle on the gridiron or the spreadsheet? Make dollars and sense.

By the time the equipment manager came out, Thornton had wrapped up his lament. He wasn't bitter or regretful, just sentimental. It was as if we all understood that change and evolution are inevitable and that the human condition is unfortunate. Football is a competitive sport but did anyone see that the real competition would be played out in the agents' and lawyers' offices…far afield from the field.

I think back on Elmer Angsman who played to be a player, not a "PLAYA!" He appreciated the game even if those who play today, don't appreciate in return. As he would put it there is no "I" in "Team" but there is in "Privilege." And to him, it was a privilege to be a player not to be a player with privilege.

--Tom

THERE'S NO PLACE LIKE HOME... A SENTIMENTAL JOURNEY!

"If these walls could talk."

It wasn't an empty sentiment, nor a cliché that was spoken by a man who hadn't been to the party, bared witness, and participated in what are now the echoes of conversations that shaped Chicago sports. It was a declaration from Bill Bidwill, the then-owner of the St. Louis Cardinals—formerly the Chicago Cardinals. The Cardinals had been in the Bidwell family since the 1930s and had gone through a strategic fight in their Chicago days to move the team from Comiskey Park to lay claim to a spot at Soldier Field. The Bears, owned originally by the Halas family were playing in those early days at Wrigley Field. And they too wanted to move to Soldier Field. Therein sparked a legendary Chicago sports and family feud to last decades long.

It was all very contentious. It was all very political. But what it really came down to was scheduling and nothing more. Whose schedule fit best with the Field's availability? You see, Soldier Field is owned by the city's parks division and is run and maintained out of that department. It is not like either of the families could buy the stadium and get the upper hand in the negotiation.

But there was a perception issue playing out as well. Comiskey Park was located in the working-class section of the southside of Chicago while Wrigley Field was in the tonier, more up-scale northside. Fans were divided by social class as much as team loyalty. To play in Soldier Field would simply level the playing field on a socio-economic basis.

Attached to Soldier Field was the historic park district building, to which Bidwill was referring when talking about his historic conversations. Bidwill could see the building from his vantage point in Bears Alley and got very sentimental about the goings on at the time. Contentious and colorful as they were.

As we know, the Cardinals lost the battle which precipitated their move to St. Louis and a subsequent move to Arizona. But Chicago, at least for Bidwill, will always be home. So, on the days when the Cardinals faced the Bears, he made the special trip to be there.

It was the final season and the decision had been made to tear down old Soldier Field for a new and improved stadium. Progress, right? Yes, but it was clearly tough for Bidwill who had a lifetime of memories stored in this hallowed site. It was just him and I standing there reminiscing and I soaked it in.

Bidwill was an odd-looking man, short and stout, with a sort of jolly face not unlike the actor Burl Ives—best known for his imagery of "Frosty the Snowman". And he had a penchant for bow ties which made him seem even more grandfatherly than he probably was but, like a grandfather, he regaled me with stories from the past. He talked about the early players—when "men were men", and not about the big buck players of today. Money was an issue in the early days, as he mentioned, and many of the guys had day jobs to support their football dreams. As such, they were a rag-tag organization in which the players weren't always available for practice or team meetings. Still, the team persevered.

He talked about the conditions at Comiskey Park such as the fact that there were no laundry facilities, so the uniforms were rinsed in sink basins and hung on clotheslines in the locker rooms to dry. The poor conditions were some of the reasons he wanted to move to Soldier Field. He went on to explain the reasoning he pulled the Cardinals out of Chicago—which was a big move for a man with big stature and a big name that went back to the 1930s in the city. Those were mob days, the days of Al Capone, and the Bidwill name meant something in Chicago. He could pull strings…but clearly not the strings needed to get him to Soldier Field.

You can tear down and build new, but it is never really the same. Sure, it is better…functionally better…but are we better off, having lost a bit of our history. Thanks to Bill Bidwill, the opposing owner, I will forever have a better appreciation of the places I've called my homes away from home for now on four decades. And sometimes, it takes an outsider looking in…looking back…to remind you of that.

George Halas is gone. Bill Bidwell is gone. Old Soldier Field is gone. Physically, sure. But thanks to a very special afternoon, with a very special person, they're not really. And never will be. The walls didn't talk to me. They talked to him. And he talked to me. And now I'm talking to you. They're echoes. And echoes…never really go away.

--Tom

Before we get all teary-eyed and sentimental about something that should never have been, the tearing down of old Soldier Field, let me talk about the reality of what needed to be.

RATS!

Vermin infestation of all kinds: from stray cats to raccoons, to RATS. And I am not talking about pet-like mice-sized rats. These were the size of small dogs, and they were everywhere.

Oh, and don't think we didn't try to get rid of them. We tried dry ice. You place it in their entrances and dens, and it inevitably kills them. But the PETA people—People for the Ethical Treatment of Animals—soon got wind of this "heinous" act and put a stop to the practice, letting four-legged creatures run amok once again. We tried poison pellets. Did you know they become immune to them? We didn't. For the record, there was no plan "C", and the problem only grew worse.

Don't think we were the only people who noticed the unwanted infiltrators. V.I.P.s and players alike all complained but it all fell on deaf ears. It seemed like, over time, everyone had their own 'rat tale' to tell. And I am no exception.

Ramp 41. It was the only way for the players to get into Bears Alley. The gate for the ramp was one of these overhead rolling doors which was both electrified but had a fail-safe pull chain attached. One afternoon, I got a call…again, why me…that the gate wouldn't open.

Sure enough, pushing the electrical mechanism did nothing. After several tries, still nothing. We opted for a pull of the chain. Nothing still. The gate wouldn't budge. Finally, a couple of us took hold of the chain and gave it one almighty tug. Three of the biggest rats I had ever seen came tumbling out of the gearbox and fell on us. I don't mind admitting, it was nearly a change of underwear moment for all of us. They were huge, they were feral, and they were coming after us. RUN!

It was determined, after getting the gate open, that rats had eaten through the wiring in the gearbox and rendered the mechanism useless. Score one for the rodents.

By now, you may be wondering just who should be taking care of this problem. Remember, Soldier Field comes under the maintenance and jurisdiction of the city park district. Not the Bears organization. Not the NFL as a league. The city of Chicago takes care of Soldier Field.

So just where were the grounds crew on any given Sunday? In their world below the world. It was as if the park's people didn't know or didn't care a game was going on around them. They had an area set up below and adjacent to the stands in which, during the game, they would BBQ and, yes, plug-in old VHS decks and watch porn. It was a man cave, quite literally, with naughty calendars and posters pasted on the walls between the necessary tools and equipment, fertilizers and paints.

Once the game began, they were bounced off the field. So, what did they do? Lit up the Weber grills—ignoring the smoke creeping up through the stands—lit their cigars and took in their porn. Oh, they'd get back to work, in their own time, when the game was over, and the stands were empty, and they could tend to the field when they were good and ready.

About that rat problem in the meantime? Hmm? Between the BBQ and the babes, who had time for rats?

Those were your city tax dollars at work. And like most seasons with the Bears, the opposing team—in this case, the rats—was winning.

--Tom

Speaking of game over, the last game played at old Soldier Field was against the Philadelphia Eagles. It was January 2001. The game was not as significant as the day was. It was the end of an era. And you could feel a palpable sense that things, as we knew them, were coming to an end. But there was also a feeling in the air of anticipation. Because when it was over, the frenzy was about to begin.

We had been told by the supervisors that when everyone was gone, namely the bosses, and the last bus had pulled away, the power would be cut off at the field four hours later. This was a wink to all the employees there that there was a four-hour window to "do what you want" in terms of stripping the place and souvenir hunting.

As a rabid collector, this was a golden opportunity for me. Or so I thought. I still had a job to do—get the players to their buses and out of the stadium. Within that time, other employees were already tearing the place to shreds. People armed with ratchet sets were unbolting the stadium seating, while those who worked in or near the skyboxes were already meticulously going from box to box grabbing what they could. So much for honor amongst thieves. Would anything be left by the time my foraging could begin?

I needed a game plan, to see what was left and what was really worth having. When the Philadelphia team finally boarded the bus and pulled away, I ran to the skyboxes to see what remained. People were literally pulling the numbers off the doors in the hallways. Nothing was sacred. And everything was wanted.

I did take a moment to look around. These boxes really were so modest by today's standards. Sure, they provided a function of keeping the necessary folk corralled away from the crowds. But luxurious was hardly a descriptor I would use. So blandly painted. So sparsely furnished. Even in their simplicity, they could have done more to make them special. I wondered if other stadiums of the day were equally meager and the want to tear down and build new was less about field improvement as it was about the creature comforts of the owners and V.I.P.s. Money talks, after all.

In one of the owner's boxes, I spotted two framed pictures still on the wall. They depicted the history of the Bears through the ages. Those I wanted but could only grab one. My friend Tim grabbed the other and we headed for the hall.

All of a sudden, I hear "STOP!" from behind me. It was a woman I recognized who was high up in the Bears' organization. She had no real authority to stop Tim or me, so Tim just kept going. I, for the right or wrong of it, chose to stop. She demanded the picture, and I handed it over. Not that she had any more right to claim it than I did, but, doing some quick analysis in my head, determined you never knew whom she knows in the organization and how these things could come back to hurt you. Ironically, she wasn't hired back at the new stadium, and it was all for naught. I was out of my picture, and she was out of a job.

But don't think I left empty-handed. I left with one of my life's prized possessions. While I was making my way through Bears Alley as I joined the initial frenzy, my eye caught something I had passed time and again, game in and game out. The Bears Alley sign. A large five-foot metal plaque that simply said it all. That, I knew I needed to have. There were two, in fact, one at each end of the Alley, and I don't know what happened to the other one. But I am grateful for mine.

I look at it, occasionally, and think to myself of days gone by, the way things used to be, and then think of old man Bidwill and chuckle to myself and simply say: "If that sign could talk."

And yes Mr. Bidwill…it speaks volumes. Old Soldier Field is gone…but is it?

--Tom

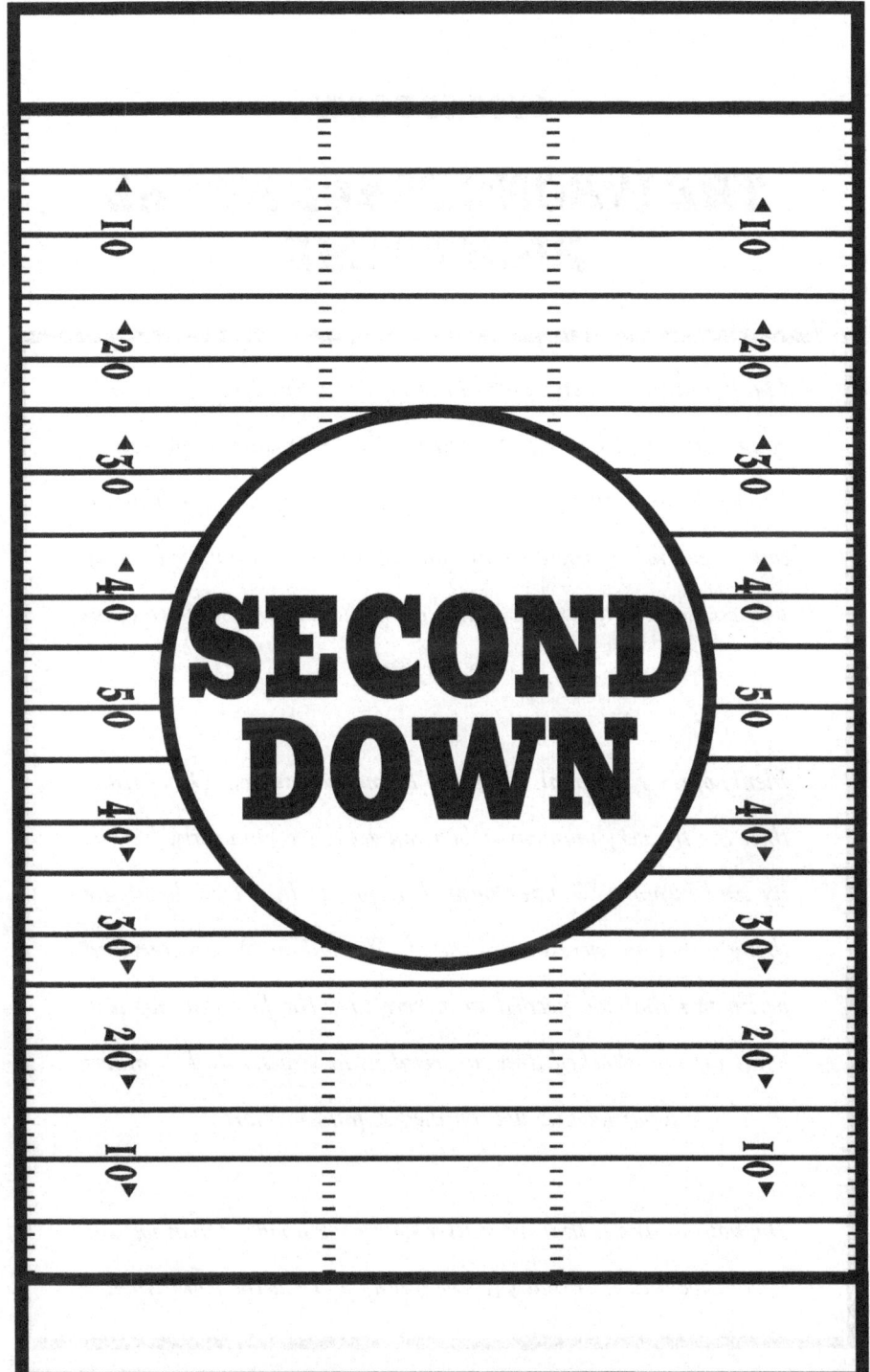

- SECOND DOWN -
THE WRONG PLACE AT THE RIGHT TIME

Having access is a curse and blessing. You see plenty but should you be looking, listening? Sometimes these moments are private... or should be. There can be guilt in knowing too much about someone. And yet there we are for one reason or another bearing witness, sometimes in the center of the action and sometimes on the sidelines.

Plenty of these moments proved to be misadventures. Other times these are the very moments when you get to see humanity, humility, and humor. We have been there for it all. Please be aware though, that our access was limited. We had our parameters and perimeters that we needed to adhere to. The fact that we saw what we saw shocked and surprised us at times...and at others what we saw was banked as fond memories.

The bottom line is that no matter where we stood...when we did what we did, it's usually in the wrong place at the right time.

MINING FOR GOLD... ONE MAN'S TRASH... IS MY TREASURE!

Balls. Footballs. The two are not mutually exclusive.

It takes balls…to get balls…it did, and I did. Who would notice if a football or two went missing over a game or two over time? That was my misguided justification for helping myself over the years. Let me make one thing clear, it was not like these coveted treasures were just sitting around for the taking. Game balls are a precious commodity and well protected. And I didn't just grab and go. But more of that in a moment.

Long before "Deflate Gate"—the Patriots scandal when accusations flew that Tom Brady was having game footballs tampered with and deflated to give him an unfair advantage during the game—footballs were allocated, assigned, and "guarded" before and during the game. There were and are protocols in place for handling the balls and not just anyone has access to them at any given moment. And just because I wanted one doesn't mean I could have one. Which made my want for one all the greater.

I would not just consider myself a fan of the game. I think of myself as a superfan. I love collecting stuff…all kinds of stuff. From the baseball caps worn by coaches, players, or teammates of any sort; to the discarded wristbands, sweaty tee shirts, socks…you name it…one man's trash was always my treasure. It wasn't that I was looking to sell the collectibles for profit. I just wanted to have what I considered a piece of sports history—legacy items if you will. Some items were harder to get than others. But with my proximity to "stuff", I couldn't help myself but to take advantage of the treasure trove of trash that potentially lay all around me.

Game day programs were discarded all over the stadium and they were easy to pick up if that was your thing. More valued items like getting a baseball cap required an ask to a player or coach or team worker and that was harder to do. I remember asking the newly formed Tampa Bay Buccaneers coach if he would mind "donating" his cap and his response was a flat-out "NO!" He wasn't being a jerk, it's just that the Bucs were a new team and didn't have money. They simply didn't have the budget to replace the baseball caps, so there was no giving them out to fans or collectors like me. Needless to say, getting one…or something with the Buccaneers logo…became a top priority for me.

If it was hard to get a cap, imagine getting your hands on a ball. As a result of "Deflate Gate", these days game balls may as well have become gold bars in Fort Knox. No one is going to touch the footballs. But in the days when I had my eyes on the prize, security was not so tight. At the Bears organization, there were twenty-four balls assigned to a game, twelve for the first half and twelve for the second. They were loaded into two large equipment bags by the equipment manager and then handed over to the referees before the game for inspection. The refs would handle each ball independently: checking for air pressure and then wiping them down with a wet towel to make them tacky.

It was good to be friends with the locker room attendants. When the refs were done meeting, my pal and I would take the balls and toss them around the locker room. Just a couple of guys horsing around. It was harmless fun. Of course, the balls eventually had to get out to the field, which was part of the attendant's job. And in his safe hands, no one ever counted inside the bags again as to whether all twelve balls made back it into one bag or another. Insert my "wink" at this point.

Why were footballs such a fascination for me? The footballs for the NFL were not over-the-counter store-bought, toys just anyone could buy. They were designed for the league and emblazoned with the Commissioner's signature or other uniquely original design work such as logos. And over time, they changed designs and signatures, accordingly, making the next one equally as desirable. After the game, the balls were retired to the next week's practice games but were never used in subsequent games. So like the Monarch butterfly, they had a short lifespan. Is it wrong that the occasional football ended up in a plexiglass case in my study rather than a dumpster in Chicago?

Balls? It took balls…sure, but we all did it. Scrounging for collectibles, or what we thought were collectibles, in the locker rooms after the games—the equivalent of fan dumpster diving. We waited for the equipment folk to clean up and clean out and then my guys and I would have at it—checking for anything left behind in the lockers or the garbage. A big prize would have been cleats, or a player's jersey, or pants, but we never found anything as glamorous as that. We would find towels, wristbands, or gloves that we could hopefully associate with a specific player. Once, early on, I even scored an official Tampa Bay Buccaneers towel with the original logo embroidered on it. The was gold because, as I've mentioned, the team was broke, and replacing that towel must have cost them a penny or two they couldn't spare.

I don't want to say I am obsessed with all things collectible, but I must say, I can be like a child with a shiny object at times. And one of those shiny objects happened to be made of plastic. It was a game between the Bears and the Eagles but not just any game, a playoff game. And for such a game, the park service, which runs and maintains Soldier Field, creates team logo signage for the locker room doors. This was not something done for every game, but rather just for playoffs, and I became enamored with that big Eagles logo next to the visitor's locker room door. By the time the game ended, and everyone had left, I had concocted in my brain some clever and complex way to get the securely fastened logo from the wall and out to my car. Ironically, the logo was simply taped to the wall, and it popped off with a gentle tug. I unceremoniously threw it into a large garbage bag and walked to my car. Score! What I was going to do with this hulking piece of plastic from a team I don't follow would require another think altogether. But to this collector's collector, it was a score nonetheless.

You would think that by some point, I would have learned my lesson about grabbing for the sake of grabbing. It's not like we had all the time in the world to embark on these would-be scavenger hunts. Stealth and speed were key. Fortunately, the locker room was simply set up with lockers lining the walls and everything set up as an open plan and easy to view.

On one of those eventful mining adventures, after a game against the New York Giants in 1985, I came across three lockers with the assignment numbers still emblazoned across the top. Among the numbers was "56", linebacker Lawrence Taylor. He'd even gone so far as to carve his number into the wooden bench in front of the locker. Lawrence Taylor was as big as you could get at the time but also a controversial figure, so anything from his locker would be a great and valued find.

I pulled open the door of the locker and started feeling around the cubby hole section where players keep personal belongings only to pull out a brown vial with a black top on it. There is a powder inside. And my mind goes to the obvious.

"Taste it," my cohorts chant.

I press my finger inside, letting a little powder stick, and tasted it. Cocaine, I presume. There is a united gasp. Had there been drugs taken during the game?

I am not here to point the finger or implicate. Yes, Lawrence Taylor, had a self-admitted drug issue at the time. Yes, there was cocaine found in his clearly marked locker. But just like I stumbled upon it, I have no idea who put it there. I can't or won't say it was his just because it was found there. Suffice it to say, it was found there. Going up the food chain with this evidence could have only led to God knows what and having to admit to what we were doing there in the first place. And who needed that aggravation? I did what I still consider the right thing to have done. Put it back and got the hell out of there.

While I know, turning trash into treasure may be a fan's dream come true…certainly mine…I also know that everything must be in moderation. Not everyone got that memo, and the parable of 'J' was a lesson for all of us.

'J' was a great guy, great in personality and great in stature. He was a big guy, which is why he was perfect for his position—locker room guardsman for the visitors' team. No one gets in or out unless he approved. Tall, good-looking, with sandy blond hair, he could have been mistaken for one of the players but, instead, worked under the auspice of a man named Mike Marano, the head of Bears security and, by day, the head of security for Mayor Daley of the great city of Chicago.

'J' also had a day job, marketing, and impressed his clients with handouts of swag for which he was helping himself on game day. You see, there were fan giveaways at the gates for incoming ticket holders. 'J' would help himself to a case or so of whatever that giveaway merchandise was and subsequently kept what he wanted and gave the rest out to his clients. It was all cheap "merch", like bobblehead dolls and mugs, that sort of thing, but it certainly wasn't his for the taking.

And like the rest of us, 'J' too enjoyed scrounging the locker rooms for goodies after the games. The difference between him and me though, is that he would walk in with his door access while the clean-up was still happening and have an unfair time advantage over the rest of us. Time advantage or not, he wasn't supposed to be in there at all during clean-up… let alone scrounging for souvenirs.

Complaints were made by the equipment manager and J's behavior put us all in jeopardy. But his antics had been going on for years, so who was going to do anything about it?

Head of Security Mike Marano, that's who!

Enough was enough. And one day 'J' was fired. Not for the reasons you might think. You see this was Chicago. It is not that you are doing something wrong. It is that you are not sharing what you are doing.

The explanation went something like this. "'J', the problem with you is that you are less like a fifty-fifty guy and more like a seventy-thirty guy." The split of the swag was not equitable in the eyes of Marano and just like that, 'J' was gone.

The lesson learned: it may take balls to be a fanatic collector… but be careful what you wish for because just like that, you can have your "balls" cut off.

For the record…Balls! Still got 'em. Footballs…not so many.

--Chet

EAVESDROPPING... INFORMATION GATHERING OR GOSSIP-MONGERING?

Proximity is an interesting thing. Sometimes you are invisible and sometimes you are just hiding in plain sight. In either case, when you are just one of the guys, people let their guard down and will say anything as if there is some sacred code that word won't get around beyond the tight circle in which we were included. We only tell the following stories because they are examples of extremes. We are not here to verify or justify, or even validate. They are the kinds of stories that could have damaged reputations or changed the course of careers at the time if people had… if we had…chosen to run with them. We always took these stories with a healthy grain of salt or discretion when necessary. So why tell you now? They can no longer hurt anyone. They are examples of the many situations in which we were privy and as much as our job was "fun and games" …it was also a test of loyalty.

In 2002, during a pre-season game between the Denver Broncos and the Bears, Mike Shanahan, the Denver Bronco's Head Coach and General Manager, had a little chat with Bear's linebacker Brian Urlacher. We were in the temporary stadium out in Champaign at the time while old Soldier Field was being recreated into the new Soldier Field.

The Broncos had come off winning the Superbowl in 1999 with John Elway as their quarterback and Urlacher was making a name for himself on the Bears—a bit of a star you might say.

As it happened, Shanahan had a plaque on the wall of the stadium honoring him for outstanding school coach of the year for his time back when, and he was admiring it with his family when Urlacher happened to come out of the locker room close to where Shanahan was standing. This was Shanahan's opportunity.

"I'd like to see you in a Bronco's uniform," he said…or something to that effect.

Urlacher just laughed.

As I handled the visiting team, getting them to the buses and off the grounds, I happened to be standing right there when Shanahan spoke. The statement hung in the air. Was it a backhanded offer? Was it simply a compliment? Was it a fishing expedition?

Do I think he meant it? Sure. You don't throw out those kinds of compliments to opposing players arbitrarily. You don't know what they are thinking any more than they know whether you are serious. It was an opening salvo for sure.

In any case, words have meaning. And these words had a value. This was considered tampering with a player. If anyone knew what I now knew, there could be fines or worse.

I knew many people in the media at this point. It would have been very easy for me to plant a story with any number of people in the upstairs press, effectively noting that Shanahan "may have" just made an off-the-cuff offer to Urlacher to join the Broncos. Would I have been wrong? In my facts…NO. In my morals…YES.

I could have been paid a substantial amount of money for that story. But what is the price of loyalty? Shanahan could have made a costly mistake in what he said, depending on who was there to hear it. I could have made a more costly mistake by selling out my proximity. In cases like this, I get paid all right…to keep my mouth shut.

--Tom

One rather incendiary story involved a Bear football player and a Blackhawk hockey player. Why would I not name them? Because it involves spousal abuse, child custody, and battery, and those accusations are a matter for the courts. Yet again, these are the kinds of stories that can ruin careers yet seem to be freely bandied about as if it were just something said over ladies' afternoon tea.

The background is simple, the hockey player, who was at the end of his career and at the end of his marriage, allegedly beat his wife. They separated and inevitably headed for divorce court. His reputation in the locker room wasn't much better than in his home life. He wasn't well-liked all around.

Enter the football player—dynamic and at the top of his game—to start dating the damsel in distress. Things are going well for the new happy couple but not so well for the pro athlete whose tensions are high. And they hit a crescendo over the son.

The hockey player and his wife were fighting for custody. They had to meet the judge. Sitting in the offices before facing the court, the two sides sat fuming. On her side, along with the wife, sat the football player and her lawyer, and on his side the hockey player and his lawyer. It didn't take long for things to get heated, and names began to fly. The hockey player referred to his wife as a "bitch" one too many times and then fists began to fly. The football player tore into the hockey player and took him apart right there in the attorney's office.

Of course, I wasn't there. How was I to know if this was true? Was this just another example of urban myth? Oh no, it's true! You see the football player is a pal of mine. When word started surfacing that the incident occurred, I talked to him about it. He confirmed it was true. Just guys being guys…I guess.

I didn't think it was a good look for my pal, so I didn't go further with retelling the antics, and even today I am guarded with those involved. Because a bust-up like that doesn't make you a hero. It makes you a thug. Is that really what we want to think of our sports icons? So, I will just keep the names to myself and let the incident speak for itself.

--Tom

I get in the elevator to take the network producers to the broadcast booth and the conversation quickly turns to Joe Theismann and his conspicuous absence that day.

Theismann at this point in his career had comfortably segued into being a network color commentator after a stellar career, first as a college quarterback for Notre Dame and then most notably spending twelve seasons with the then-named Washington Redskins. He was in the Hall of Fame and football, if not an American, hero. By all accounts, he was affable and easy to work with—a genuinely good guy.

We are no sooner in the elevator and one producer starts on the loss of Theismann from the show run down and taps his finger on the side of his nose as an indicator as to why the loss. Now, everyone knows that tap is a signal for a cocaine issue. Was this pisher of a producer really accusing Hall of Fame great Joe Theismann of having a cocaine problem… and moreover, one so bad that he was missing broadcasts because of it? I was shocked. This was not a rumor that was circulating. Not the buzz around the stadium.

Theismann wrote in his book published in the late 80s that he drank heavily and that he gambled but he never admitted to drug use. Ironically, his son, Joe Jr., was later arrested in 2003 for selling cocaine but none of that indicates Theismann had a problem of his own.

Did he or didn't he? I don't know and I am guessing that producer didn't really know. It is dangerous to even indicate such an implication and even more so when you are talking about somebody notable. Did the producer understand the term "slander?"

When the door opened and they stepped out, I didn't feel as if I was in the "know" but rather in the "NO!" And I am not afraid to tell this story because it is not a story about whether Joe Theismann has a problem with cocaine, it is a story about whether a certain producer has a problem with Joe Theismann. You see, from where I stand, on the periphery, it is just far enough to have clear sight, not near sight. When it comes to stories like this, you'd better know the difference between the two!

--Chet

One of the most outrageous stories circulating was regarding Brett Favre and his wife Deanna.

Word had it that the couple was having trouble conceiving a baby. This can be gut-wrenching and a personal journey. When you are a personality, a sports icon, your personal journey is public curiosity. There was talk of the frustrations of invitro fertilization not working and Favre himself partying to offset those frustrations. It was press and media fodder not just hearsay.

Then there was the rape! This was not associated with Favre! Green Bay Packers tight end star Mark Chmura was arrested for sexually assaulting his former babysitter in the bathroom after a drinking game during a post-prom party in Wisconsin.

So how, as rumors go, is this linked to Favre? Well, the talk was he was partying in Milwaukee when the rape happened in Wisconsin, and not soon after Deanna was pregnant—not just pregnant, but reportedly far along in her pregnancy. The talk was, the Favres bought a baby. Was there even a rape baby? People were connecting dots. But was it fair? Was it real? It made for good gossip...the facts be damned.

You can't get more outrageous a story. People believe what they want to believe. You could conceivably connect the dots, given that the dots are really there.

Why even tell this story? Because sometimes the outrageous may actually stir outrage. You must draw the line somewhere. Even if what we hear is true, when is it our business to make it our business? Let's face it, gossip is fun. Malicious lies are dangerous. So, where is that line I drew? The fifty-yard line. Because you got a fifty-fifty shot at being right...and I don't like those odds.

I stand along the proximity. I hear what hear. Sometimes I am told directly. Sometimes I am the invisible receiver. I have told what I know but know more than I tell. And that is the way it is going to be.

Because yes, Tom and I could have made a killing, selling to the salacious side of what we've seen. There is no "I" in "greed" but there is in "proximity" …and that's what this job gives us. Proximity!

--Chet

THERE'S NO CRYING IN FOOTBALL!

You're not just running a play…running the ball, when it comes to professional football you are also running an emotional gamut. The angst is real. The frustration is real. The panic is real. Whether you are just making the leap from college to the pros or are a multi-million-dollar contract holder, the pressure to perform is great. There are high expectations on your high adrenalin and if it doesn't go right…well…that's on you! No one's going to take your hand, pat your back, or give you a hug. It's football, damn it! There's no crying in football…or is there? And watching others break down is enough to break you down.

We love our hometown heroes. Thirty-five miles or so from Chicago lies the city of Joliet, Illinois, population 150,000 on a good day and known as the "City of Stone" for reasons too uninteresting to get into. What is interesting, is what lies in the heart of this sleepy suburb: Joliet

Catholic Academy which produced Tampa Bay Buccaneers fullback Mike Alstott—from back in the day when fullbacks were still a thing. By the time he got to the Bucs/Bears game at Soldier Field, he was an Illinois state conference Hall of Famer and the homeboy who did good. Needless to say, eyes were not just on the ball but also on the boy for this Sunday's match-up.

His family was in the stands. His friends were in the stands. And as was tradition, when someone prominent was at the stadium, those family and friends were taken care of both in the stands and escorted down to Bears Alley to wait for the player or team member tucked away from the throngs of people. We had made that arrangement for the Alstott clan after the game.

Mike did a pretty good job on the field and after the game, the local press was all over him wanting to know what it was like to be back in his own backyard once again. The problem was, the Bucs had lost the game and Alstott had felt he, being the focus of the locals had particularly let the team down and looked like a loser in front of his family and friends.

Mike's story with his family was not just another proud parenting story. The Alstott family came from a humble background. Dad was a garbage collector. Even getting Mike into Joliet Catholic Academy was something of a feat. And the fact that he was there for all the games and a proud supporter of his son was the kind of story Hollywood writes about. In fact, Hollywood did make a movie much like it: "Rudy"—not about Alstott, but it might as well have been. So when the game was over, we had Dad and Mom patiently and proudly waiting by the locker room door for Mike to walk out. And then he did.

Mike is no shrinking violet. He is a big man—as you would expect a full back to be. When the door opened and he caught sight of his Dad standing about twenty feet away and at that moment, the day caught up with him, and the hulk of a fullback simply broke down.

As they hugged, Mike couldn't stop sobbing and saying: "I let you down. I let you down." His father just hugged him tight and let him cry. The comfort was real. The support was there. Nothing needed to be said. It was what his father had always been for his son…there.

I was so moved and so close, I could have hugged him myself. As a father myself, I felt for the father. But I have something bigger on my mind. On the way out, there were more than a dozen of his former teammates from Joliet Catholic waiting for him—it was to be a bit of a surprise that was set up to be a bit of a nightmare scenario under the circumstances. Clearly, he seemed to be in no mood to entertain those folks.

In fact, it proved to be just the opposite. Because for their hometown hero, it wasn't about winning the game…it was all about being in the game in the first place. A garbage man's son playing on the holy turf of Soldier Field is more than a dream come true.

Today, Alstott coaches young upstarts like the kind he once was, in a school in Florida.

I hope he remembers like I do that moment in Soldier Field and teaches that there actually may be crying in football—tears of joy—when you realize the impossible has become possible.

--Tom

There is nothing worse than being a great player on a losing team...or should I say a team of losers. That's what Barry Sanders seemed to be feeling, playing for the Detroit Lions. As a running back, he led the league in rushing yardage during several seasons, despite only being 5' 8" and just over 200 pounds. Pound for pound, he was worth his weight in agility. But as his career wound down, so did the Detroit Lions as an organization. He was still a star while the Lions' star had long since faded. Again, everyone knows, there is no "I" in "team" but there is in "island." That is pretty much what he was by the late 1990s, an island, and taking on water. And he was not happy about it...pissed is the better term.

So, around 1997, I was able to see just how pissed a player can get when Sanders and the Lions came to play the Bears. I don't have to tell you, the Lions lost. By the time, it was time to leave the stadium Barry was nowhere to be found. The press, the media, the fans, and fellow teammates on the bus were waiting and not so patiently. Still, there was simply no Barry.

Except I knew where he was. He was still in the locker room... crying...a near fit of hysteria. He had had enough. He was frustrated and humiliated—having done his part only to be let down by a team, again, who couldn't seem to get it together. He could see the writing on the wall. To get off this team, he would have to get out of football. And in doing that he would be tainted by the other losers he called teammates. Rather than going out in a blaze of glory, he feared a whimper, not a bang. He had the right to fear what seemed to be inevitable.

It was humbling to know a man of great perception could be taken down like this. He just sat there crying but it wasn't my place to intercede. But the more it went on, the more questions were being asked and answers were being expected. He needed his time. But time was ticking, forty minutes and counting. So, we went in.

"I can't go out there," he sobbed.

It was true. He certainly couldn't go out there in the state he was in. But the bottom line was he couldn't stay where he was for much longer. A plan was hatched to take him out the equipment room door, out the backway, bypass those waiting, and get him on the team bus. My brother Tom was to do the escorting. Despite being dressed in a hoodie, with the hood up covering his head, people did recognize him and shouted for autographs and pictures. The best-made plans aren't always the best-laid plans, but he got to the bus, even if he looked a little uncaring to the smattering of fans left wanting.

He retired a couple of seasons later, which was no surprise to me. Fortunately, his reputation as a stellar player remains intact. As for me, I will never forget that day, witnessing the human behind the hero and personification of the oft-used phrase: the bigger they are, the harder they fall.

These players have both pressures placed on them and place pressure on themselves. We want to believe they are somehow superhuman… that's SUPER human. Now, remembering back on this one instance, with this one player…I can think of so many others that I have witnessed and talked with who have come to realize they too are super, yes, but human first.

--Chet

When they were building the new Soldier Field, we had been relegated to Champaign to the college stadium out there. It served its purpose, but the configuration was very different from what we had been used to back in Chicago—everything from its horseshoe shape to the way the lockers were laid out made us rethink the way we did our jobs.

To get the coaches to the coach's box, we essentially went out a back door of the locker room and down a concourse to the elevator and then on up to the boxes. Okay, it was a little convoluted but once I figured it out…it was the way it was. My way to get to the coach's locker room was to cut through the player's locker room. Again, so be it.

On this one Sunday, we were playing the Denver Broncos. I was on my way through the locker room, doing my routine, when I couldn't help but notice one of the quarterbacks—a second-string guy—all suited up but going nowhere. He was simply pacing back and forth and mumbling to himself.

"I can't do it. I can't do it," he repeated over and over again. "I can't go out there. I can't go out there. I just can't do it."

He was genuinely frightened enough to have me concerned.

I caught the eye of the coach across the room who now knows I see what he sees. The coach is doing nothing. The player is clearly having a full-blown panic attack and, again, no one is stepping in to help.

The coach ambles over to me. "You see what's happening?"

"Yeah," I return almost pleading with him to intervene.

"This happens more than you think," he begins as if to say it's nothing to worry about. He continues as if he owes me some kind of explanation. "Think about it. He probably started playing football around 7 or 8 years old. And then he goes to high school where he starts to excel. By his senior year, he is recruited for college. He does well at one of the big colleges which leads to the NFL draft. He sits on the bench for one or two seasons until this opportunity plays out. He's a Bronco. It's his first game as a pro. Now what? Of course, he has the jitters."

This was far more than the jitters. I am no psychologist but even I could see that. This kid has found himself on a winning NFL team and despite all his training and preparation, is he mentally ready? Clearly not, if he is damn near catatonic and chanting that he "can't do it." And he was just on the second string.

If you think about these multi-million-dollar newcomers like Patrick Mahomes, the pressure to be worth your paycheck has got to be staggering. Granted Mahomes is the son of a professional athlete, a baseball player for the Yankees, so he was probably comfortable around the locker room and the expectations of turning professional. Still, the pressure to perform on his level can be crushing to and for the average Joe.

The coach could not have been more nonplussed by the antics of his newbie Bronco and let him pace it out until he faced his demons. All totaled, that took a relatively short ten minutes or so. The kid left for the field and nothing more was spoken. I felt bad. Not just for the kid but for the state of that kind of leadership. Isn't a coach supposed to do just that, coach? Doesn't that include talking your player off the ledge when necessary? Could it have been that he just wasn't high enough up the food chain to matter? Let's face it, he was just the second string. He was no Patrick Mahomes.

But just like injuries on the field or concussion protocols, should there be some consideration for psychological trauma? Or is that just all in MY head? What does that say about how disposable players really are? Just a thought…about thoughts.

--Tom

DAMNED IF YOU DID

It didn't get more political than this. Colin Kaepernick, the highly visible quarterback for the San Francisco 49ers took a knee in 2016 during the national anthem stating that he could not stand for pride in the flag of a nation that oppressed black people. This simple gesture rippled across the hearts and minds of the players and the teams the league over. And before you knew it, you were damned if you did and damned if you didn't.

So how did I get caught up in this situation? I am neither a player nor a team official. Yet there I was front and center in one of the most controversial player decisions of this controversy.

The night before the entire moment, Donald Trump made a comment about the players who were continuing to take a knee. And as only Donald Trump can be, the comment was colorful and disparaging to the players, clearly missing the point of the messaging, and only looked at the gesture as being un-American. But it hit a nerve within the NFL. Each of the teams had been called by the Commissioner with a request that each team had to submit a declaration of intent as to what the team would be doing during the national anthem on the following Sunday. Make no mistake, this was a big deal. The NFL was convinced that should any player, any team, misstep on this issue there could be rioting from the fans in the stands.

That Sunday, the Bears were playing the Steelers. It had been decided by the Bears organization that when the national anthem was playing, the players would simply stand in a line formation and lock arms. It was a show of apolitical unity…or so it was to be interpreted. The Steelers on the other hand had decided they would stay in the locker room for the playing of the anthem.

The decision not to come out of the locker room at all was itself controversial. The national media wanted to know why the team had chosen to take that stance and during pregame interviews, it was clarified in statements saying something to the effect that they believed in not coming to the field at all, they were not making any political statement that could be misconstrued or misinterpreted in any way. They were simply avoiding the issue altogether.

By not letting the players out onto the field, the atmosphere in the tunnel was insane. The players were at a fever pitch, pounding walls, yelling, and jumping up and down. I had already gotten the coaches to their respective boxes and made my way back to the tunnel when they were close to starting the national anthem. Then everything stopped. It is weird. No one was doing anything. The frenzy in the tunnel simply died.

With that, number 78 steps through the crowd and forward to the front of the tunnel. He turns to Steve Goodwin—the man in communication with the television network who inevitably would get the okay to let the men out of the tunnel and onto the field for the television cameras—and asks when they are going to start singing the anthem.

"In about 15 seconds."

He walked past me to get to Steve and instinctively I followed behind him. Cameras, both still and video, were lined up in front of him. He walked toward the field and got just to the edge with me in tow when the anthem began. I stood frozen. Cameras to the Ballard brothers? We're like moths to a flame. If this was a big enough gesture on 78's part to attract this much attention from the media, I wasn't going anywhere.

Just who is number 78? Offensive tackle, Alejandro Villanueva who stands on the top end of the six-foot spectrum and was not shy of one side or the other of three hundred pounds. He began his football career playing in college for the Army Black Knights and in fulfilling his army duties won a Bronze star as an Army Ranger and served three tours of duty in Afghanistan. If he was badass on the field of duty, you can imagine what he was like on the football field.

Needless to say, the national anthem meant a little something to Villanueva. And when they started singing, he simply stopped and put his hand over his heart. If there was ever a player who deserved to be front and center for the anthem it was this guy and he had to break with his team to do it. And there I am standing right behind him. Now, I mention this because as the anthem began my phone started blowing up in my pocket. Constant buzzing as it was on vibrate. I just stood there with my hand on my heart as well.

When the anthem was over, it was like the running of the bulls in Spain with the players racing for the field. I retreated to the locker room area to find out what the phone blast was all about. I was on television! It seems the moment with Villanueva was broadcast everywhere and the pictures subsequently made national and international headlines. My fifteen minutes of peripheral fame time clock was ticking. For the record, I did catch myself the next day on GOOD MORNING AMERICA. The Ballard big time!

After selfishly basking in a glory that wasn't my own, I heard the sobering news that Villanueva actually apologized to his team later for breaking ranks and doing what could only be seen as something patriotic and a personal statement from a bona fide war hero. Is that what we've become? What this nation has become? You have to apologize for being a patriotic hero but I get all kinds of praise for standing in the background photobombing the moment. God bless America!

I did run into number 78 when the action calmed down, told him I was standing in the proximity of the scene and that I appreciated what he had done. He, in turn, appreciated my words. I felt embarrassed for having been there for what seems in hindsight selfish reasons and yet grateful for having witnessed social history.

With all due respect to Colin Kaepernick and his right to make his statement—a statement that was non-violent, personal, and used his celebrity for positive messaging—I have to applaud Alejandro Villanueva for serving his country before politicizing his country. He's earned the right to stand proud for pure reasons when others chose to cower from controversy. A hero indeed.

And I am proud to have been there in the moment—all jokes aside as to whether I was there accidentally or egotistically—I quite literally stood behind a brave man who took his bravery one step further that day. I stood behind him literally…but I stand behind him in every other way.

--Tom

PARANOIA CAN DESTROY YA!

Ed Hochuli is one of the most recognizable referees in the NFL for two reasons. One, his tight jerseys showed off his well-maintained physique. Two, the penchant for over-explaining the reasoning behind his penalty calls. I, on the other hand, remember him for one other reason. A phobia…and I will explain.

Now you must understand, the referee is the most guarded of all animals in the jungle that is the NFL. They are not to be talked to—as in interviewed or second-guessed. Their decisions are sacred and final. They, it seems, have ultimate power. So, what they say goes.

You should also know that prior to the start of the game, there are a series of meetings that occur in the order of the minutes counting down to the game: the 100-minute meeting—with security and the local cops, the 90-minute meeting—with the public relations people, and the 60-minute meeting—with the referees and the medical team. It is during that meeting that the discussion turns to logistics—the "what if's." If anything were to go wrong in the game or with the game, it is the ref's judgment as to whether to stop the game. It is a huge responsibility and, on this day, Hochuli being the big cheese, such responsibility would be his. The cheese stands alone.

By this time, into the new millennium, broadcasting had advanced. The use of drones had been implemented for new and better camera angles. But they were still a new technology and clearly not embraced by all. Certainly not Hochuli. But television drones were not the issue…drones collectively were.

The meeting took place in the alley, so I was privy to the conversation as it happened. As the guys were talking logistics, the usual stuff, Hochuli piped up with, "What are we going to do about the drones?"

Soldier Field was open air. His point was that anyone with a drone could fly it into the stadium at any time and disrupt the game, gather illegal footage, or worse.

People stood silent. What about the drones? No one really knew how to defend against a potential drone invasion. He got more adamant.

"I'm deathly afraid of what drones can do," he continued. "I'm telling you right now, if a drone flies into the field, I am stopping the game. I am going to direct my crew and everyone off the field."

He literally felt drones were bomb-carrying weapons of mass destruction and would not have any part of it.

Yes, he seemed like a paranoid fool. And, yes, he made us all paranoid for the whole of the game. Even a pigeon could make us jump.

There was nothing we do about it but duck for cover and hope for the best—one eye on the field and one toward the skies.

His rantings may have been heard though. Today there are protocols in place for the unexpected drone. Security doesn't allow me to tell exactly how they deal with the pesky predators but suffice it to say they'd be downed faster than they go up.

But if you think a tiny drone got one ref rattled, nothing beats Patriots owner Robert Kraft demanding the FAA down flights for a game with the Bears in Champaign post-9/11.

That's right. Of course, you would think that a billionaire owner of one of the most winning teams in the NFL, the New England Patriots, and the holder of six Super Bowl rings would get what he wanted. After all, terrorist threat paranoia post-9/11 is a very real thing. In this case, the sum of money and power didn't add up to the answer for which he was looking.

Now, you must understand that Champaign, Illinois, is farm country. There are crop dusters flying all the time. No harm, no foul. We, the Bears, were really the interlopers for the time were borrowing the university stadium while the new Soldier Field was being built. The least we could be was accommodating. Bob Kraft didn't see it that way.

As we walked the field during warm-up, Kraft looked in the sky and notices a small aircraft in the distance. "Where did that plane come from?" he asked, more ignorant than bombastic. "This is supposed to be a no-fly zone…like at any stadium."

I tried to explain that it was just a crop duster that was more than likely finishing for the day…but…he wanted the FAA called and all flights grounded.

We were forty-five minutes before kickoff and with all due respect to Mr. Kraft and the rules, I didn't have a clue who to call and on such short notice.

I stood for a moment to take him in. Dapper, with his gray hair and welcoming smile. He was in his traditional suit and tie—a disarming pink tie—looking like the Bob Kraft, the owner, that he always presented himself to be. There was no sign of eccentricity. He wasn't even demanding, just insistent. I chuckled to myself and swallowed hard, knowing his "request" was never going to happen, and spent the rest of the game hoping to the heavens as I stared at the heavens that all planes had landed safely, and my job was…well...grounded.

--Tom

It was a Monday night game in Champaign and the Bears were playing the Green Bay Packers. Just as the buses with the players and coaches pulled up, Red, the equipment manager for the Packers pulled me aside. He was seemingly flustered.

"Tom, you have to come with me and get all the furniture out of the coaches' office" he asked…no insisted.

"What are you talking about?"

"They're concerned about being bugged!"

There is a long-time, ongoing, rivalry between the Bears and the Packers. That is for sure. The fans love it. The players play for it. And I suppose part of that rivalry is that no one trusts each other. But in all the years this has been going on, I had never heard of any sort of backstage cheating or double-crossing like this. Bugging…the furniture!

The Packers don't have an owner. They have a Board of Directors. As such, it was my belief that the directive came directly from the coaches themselves. Okay, so be it. They would get what they wanted. I had to wonder if this would be the standard from then on. (It wouldn't be.)

Remember, this was Champaign, the university stadium, and the set-up was nothing elaborate. There was just a chair, a couch, and a love-seat which we quickly pulled out and placed outside by the door while everyone was getting off the bus.

Brett Favre threw one of those magnificent fifty-plus yard tosses, found his man, and as part of that the Packers won the game. The rivalry continues.

I was never told what was really "bugging" the coaches that day. I hope they were happy, as they now had nothing to sit on. Ironically, we did…and did!

--Tom

When wearing my "Chief" hat, I had a lot of leeway as to where I went and what I did, and no one really questioned me. People, even my co-workers who should have known better, assumed I was some sort of

"Chief." Chief of what? They never asked and I never corrected them. Win/Win! Certainly, I did my job, escorting the visiting coaches, but that inevitably left a lot of time during the game to point myself in any number of directions. Like every fan in the stadium, I just simply wanted to see the game and sought out a spot with the best vantage point.

I often sat with the coaches in their box. It made sense—a bird's eye view and "Johnny-on-the-spot" if need be. I always had an excuse to be there. "Just in case you need something at the last minute…" or "What if you need an escort?" For the most part, it worked. I minded my business, and I stayed out of theirs. But this time it was Super Bowl season, tensions were high, and I may have been in the wrong place at the wrong time.

The Bears were playing the Minnesota Vikings. I, of course, was in the visiting coaches' box. As everyone is getting settled, I ask the obvious, "Does anyone need anything?" I should have just kept my mouth shut.

Pete Carroll turns to me and without missing a beat blurts out, "Yeah, I need you to leave."

I was stunned. There was no explanation and I felt like a little boy who had just disappointed his parents. I was there by his good graces and there was nothing I could say.

Carroll has gone on to be one of the most respected coaches in all of football and one of only three to win a Super Bowl and a college national championship, but back then he was the defensive coach for the Vikings. At that moment, all I was concerned about was that I was busted, but why?

"Okay," was the best I could muster, and headed for the door.

It wasn't like he was being nasty, but it was clear he wanted me out. Was I some sort of a spy? Was I some sort of a distraction? I got the directive and left.

Pete Carroll proved to be one of the most confident men to ever lead men in the game. So, I often look back on that moment and wonder what kind of threat I could possibly have posed. Perhaps none…until I was one. And that is called strategy. Strategy wins games. Pete Carroll wins games. The "Chief" was out! Not for good…for his good.

--Chet

UP IN SMOKE: WHEN YOU JUST DON'T GIVE A PISS... LITERALLY!

In the immediate years after 1985 and the Super Bowl win, the team players were Gods. They were making appearances, doing television commercials—even had a music video out. You may have thought it would have all gone to their heads and there would have been no talking to them, let alone fraternization. But no. They were part of our little tribe and they, in turn, treated us like part of the team.

Traditionally, when you come to a big national game, part of the fun is the tailgate—when attendees set up the BBQ or picnic spreads out of the back of their cars in the parking lot and party pre-game. That was not an option for us working stiffs. For us, working the game, we would have something I like to call the "end-game"—a post-party—which inevitably took place in the player's parking garage. Leftover food—and no, not that damn Brown's chicken—was brought down from the sky boxes.

(The V.I.P. boxes had catered spreads and those in charge of ordering the amount of food for those boxes always ordered far more than necessary for the V.I.P.s in order to cater to our needs later on. We appreciated them for that.) The leftovers, which were always a substantial amount, coupled with whatever we brought in ourselves made for quite an impressive spread each week.

Make no mistake, these little gatherings were no little gatherings. On any given Sunday, we, my immediate gang, could expect to rub elbows with up to and around forty others—from different departments and including the players themselves. Some players stayed and hung out and others offered a cordial nod or hello and then got in their cars and headed out. It was a regular thing but very informal. Cocktails and beers were flowing, and the conversation was light and breezy. It was everyone just having one collective exhale after the game. It was great to be part of, a collective bonding, which quite literally leveled the playing field between those being hero-worshiped and us, the supporting players. These moments were the great equalizers.

One Sunday I got the nod from a player to follow him down and around to a more secluded area of the lot. I thought there would be an exchange of some gossip, a story not to be shared with just anyone or broadcast throughout the festivities. There were about four of us there. Standing next to the player, I noticed how relatively small he was compared to the other players. That was neither here nor there, just an observation I made as I waited for the story to begin. There was no story. Out of nowhere, a marijuana joint was produced, lit, and passed around.

It's not like a joint was hardcore, but drugs were still drugs, back then especially. And the league had standards—strict standards and protocols. Clearly, the player was aware of this and the need for privacy. After all, we weren't standing in the middle of the garage lighting up, for all the team to see. There was a reason we were ensconced in the bowels, out of sight, discreetly tucked away.

As the player took his hit, I could see a career—a Super Bowl-winning career—going up in smoke, literally. Yet he didn't seem to give a shit…or as it turned out a piss.

I stood for a while and mused on what was happening, thought about what I would do in his circumstance, and couldn't help myself but to turn to him and ask: "What happens if tomorrow the NFL comes to you and says we need to drug test you?"

Perhaps I was crossing the line. The looks on the other faces may have said I was, I don't know. But I had to know. Was this guy really ready to jeopardize his entire career over a toke from a joint?

With that came the answer I wasn't ready for, "Well, that's no problem. Because I'll just get some piss from a guy that doesn't smoke." Issue closed.

A situation like that never arose again, not with that player, and not with other players. Perhaps I had been ostracized for asking the question and crossing the line. But over the years it nagged at me, his answer.

Was it entitlement? Was it arrogance? He was blatantly breaking the rules—or at least knew how to sidestep them—because he knew he could. That, to me, is not a team player. You owe something to the team that put you in a privileged position, not willing to risk it and let them down because you know how to break the rules. I am no puritan and, yes, I was there participating too during that evening. But I had a hell of a lot less on the line. And yes, the story has made for good cocktail conversations over the years.

I have chosen not to name him for several reasons: He still works and I don't want to sully his reputation. Moreover, it is not for me to stand on a moral high ground. As I said, I participated too. But I will say this about that. On a winning team, as the Bears were, I expected to be in the presence of nothing but winners.

--Chet

THE FOG OF WAR... OR WAS IT JUST A GAME OF BLIND MAN'S BLUFF?

They wanted to play, both, the head coaches on either side. So, when they discussed with officiating referee Jim Tunney, who made the call "upstairs", it was decided the game would go on. Tunney's own criteria were that his refs could see both goalposts, which was enough for the game to continue—a declaration that was collectively contradicted by most on the field. The problem was no one could see. The fog had rolled in at 12:55 p.m. central standard time, for the start of the second half of one of the most contentious playoff games in football to date, blinding everyone—from the refs to the players, to the coaches, to the 65,000 fans in the stands, and to the millions watching at home. What started out as the Philadelphia Eagles versus the Chicago Bears...or more importantly the head coaches Buddy Ryan versus Mike Ditka playoff...turned into a legendary Act of God known as "The Fog Bowl." And the Ballard brothers were there—New Year's Eve, 1988.

It was hard to say we were eyewitnesses to history as the fog was so thick, as mentioned, no one could see. But I, Chet, was positioned in my usual spot with the coaches and I, Tom, was along the sidelines manning security to make sure unruly fans didn't storm the field. Neither of us had an advantage, just proximity to what became "the greatest game no one saw."

It is important to understand just how important the significance of this game really was and for that, you must go back just over three years. Ryan and Ditka were both on the coaching staff of the Bears—Ryan was the defensive coach and Ditka was the head coach. Now, ordinarily, Ryan would have been answerable to Ditka. This is where it gets tricky. George Halas, the then-owner of the Bears, had given Ryan an iron-clad contract whereby he was answerable to no one in all critical decision-making, including the head coach, and because of this, his coaching decisions were absolute and final. As you can imagine, this created immense tension between Ryan and the always-bombastic Ditka who liked to leave his thumbprint all over the team.

By 1985, this coaching rivalry hit hurricane force—neither were speaking to each other but had plenty to say about each other--despite together leading the team to be the Superbowl-winning Bears. In so doing, Ryan saw his chance to exit in a blaze of glory to the Eagles grabbing the mantle of head coach.

There was no graciousness left behind. After his defection, when asked what he thought Ditka thought of his defection, Ryan's only reply was, "Mike who?"

It was inevitable the two head coaches would go head-to-head. Yet, even then, the rivalry got the better of anything that smacked of a civil match. For their first game against one another it was commented with great fanfare that Ryan "looked good in green", the Eagles team colors, and upon the game finish, rather than shake hands Ryan ran to the locker room to avoid the traditional gentleman's acknowledgment.

Having gone through 1986 and 87 without repeating the performance from 1985, Ditka and the Bears were chomping at the bit to get to the Superbowl. As it turned out, the only thing standing in the way was Buddy Ryan and the Eagles and one playoff game. They were to meet at Soldier Field on New Year's Eve 1988. And the war of the words began. "He's nothing but an empty tin can," Ditka began about Ryan.

Despite the Bears being favored over the Eagles, Buddy, for his part, was making his presence known—circling the team buses around Soldier Field three times with horns blaring, making sure everyone knew Buddy Ryan was there to battle.

The day started out sunny and crisp and favored the Bears for the first half, ending with Chicago in the lead 17-6. And then it started—something defensive tackle Dan Hampton was quoted as calling a "Biblical Pestilence" rolled in. And rolled in it did, up and over the walls of the stadium like a blanket coming off Lake Michigan.

It was called advective fog—a rare phenomenon for sure—whereby the warm air from the Lake that morning was blown inland and hit the cooler air within the stadium. The result was the creation of prism-like micro-droplets which reflected light and caused a whiteout condition. Ironically, just two miles away, this lake effect phenomenon was not happening at Comiskey Park nor was it happening at the airport or disrupting flights at O'Hare. It was simply a Soldier Field occurrence.

Should the game have been called…or at the very least suspended? According to most people who were there, but Jim Tunny, as mentioned, continued the game. Players claimed to be able to see ten feet, and the refs admitted to ten yards. The coaches on the sidelines had no idea of plays being called or what was inevitably being played. Mike Singletary admitted publicly that he could not confirm with the coordinator and simply wondered about the plays that were being called. Still, they continued to march into the mist and not just with a running game. The Eagles' quarterback, Randall Cunningham, threw for a remarkable four hundred yards. The Bears intercepted three times. Field goals were attempted and made. And no one could tell just how many flags should have been thrown and mistakes missed.

I, Chet, being with coaches did get to see pure frustration play out—and it was hardly the game anyone anticipated. Somehow both sides accepted the fate of the situation. Buddy Ryan summed it up best when he said, "The same fog was on my side as it was on their side." So all seemed fair. But from where I stood, it didn't make for the playoff everyone was looking forward to. Even though the Bears were winning, no one seemed to understand "how".

I, Tom, spent the game coordinating security along the sidelines making sure fans didn't take advantage of the opportunity to race the field. I spent the afternoon running up and down the field trying to follow the ball, and radioing back my location to the rest of the security team. It was said, that following us allowed some team members and/or officials to follow the game. Maybe, maybe not. It was little more than a game of blind man's bluff.

The Bears did take the game. It was considered by many to be an accidental win as people believed the real reason the game was not called was that there was too much at stake in the advertising dollars. Quite simply, the CBS network had too much money on the line. That too was angry speculation. Ironically, the fog lifted as soon as the game was over. If they had just postponed, like so many had called for, perhaps things would have turned out differently.

It was hard to pat himself on the back for a lopsided win under the conditions of the win. Still, Ditka went public with the statement, sticking it to Ryan: "When you make things personal, you've got a problem." Even he had to laugh at the ludicrousness of his own attack. For the record, the momentum of the win didn't last. The Bears were shut out for the next games and, thereby, shut out of their Superbowl dreams.

As far as the Ballard brothers. Yet again, overall, we can say we were there for history, we were part of history, but like everyone who was there that day...or tuned in at home for that matter...we didn't get to "Bear" witness to history.

--Chet & Tom

SOME PLAYERS CAN BE REAL D*CKS!

You can imagine the atmosphere in a locker room. Men being men. Towel snapping. Dirty jokes. Foul language. Blowing off steam. After the game it was not uncommon for the players to mess with the press, especially the ladies of the media, and have their shower towels accidentally open or even fall off—exposing their prowess off the field. A certain GOAT in the league, for instance, would talk about his favorite receiver who had a penchant for walking around the locker room in the altogether because he was altogether positive that people would be impressed with what he had on display. Sure, there are rules for propriety, but these guys are what the term is today: "Ballers"—on so many levels. Those "gifted" were more likely to play the game, naturally. The problem got so bad that the Bears issued Velcro shower towels to mitigate the slippage issue. But a splaying leg to a visiting reporter could easily change the direction of one's eye line. Men can be pigs…or so it's been said.

We Ballard brothers have seen this in action and do get asked about it every once in a while, but as we never really paid much attention to the antics, we had little to say. Until, one day, back at old Soldier Field, when even we were taken aback by one player's gift which turned out for another employee, to be the gift that kept on giving.

It was a Packers game and Tom and I happened to be standing near one another by the visiting player's gate onto the field before the players emerged. But Tom wandered off by the time the players were making their way to the field.

A few minutes later, as the players were rushing past, I happened to notice one of the Packers was clearly packing. At this point, it is worth noting the players, for the most part, don't wear any protection…down there…leaving a clear outline of whatever weaponry they may be sporting. And like most, this particular Packer wasn't wearing a protective cup. That wasn't unusual. But he was…unusual that is. I signal to my brother, indicated his number, and mentioned the enormity of his manhood.

Please understand, as someone who is non-plussed by such things, to be shocked as I was, is a good indicator of what I had witnessed. Tom made his way around and back with a similar shock and awe assessment. The conversation was all about this player and what a player he must be.

We didn't notice that we were being overheard by one of the staff manning the gate. After the rest of the players ran out onto the field, the gatekeeper ran over to us.

"I couldn't help but overhear what you were talking about," he began excitedly. "I saw it too…and now I can't stop staring at all the c*cks on all the players. I'm obsessed."

Okay? The power of the penis? The question now is when you are sitting on the couch, on a Sunday afternoon, watching the game, will you sneak a peek?

It just goes to show you. Some players are real d*cks and some players are just cocky!

--Chet

P.S. The Lord giveth and the Lord taketh away!

There is a certain staff member of a certain Houston team. A short and portly man who also has a penchant for walking around the locker room naked. The irony is twofold. First, he is not a player. So, there is no reason for him to be showering with the players and therefore to be naked at all. Second, he has what is kindly referred to as a micro-penis. There are no bragging rights to be had and, in fact, takes a great deal of ribbing for his shortcomings. So, yet again, the players are being d*cks…about a d*ck!

Then again, everyone loves a good d*ck joke!

--Chet

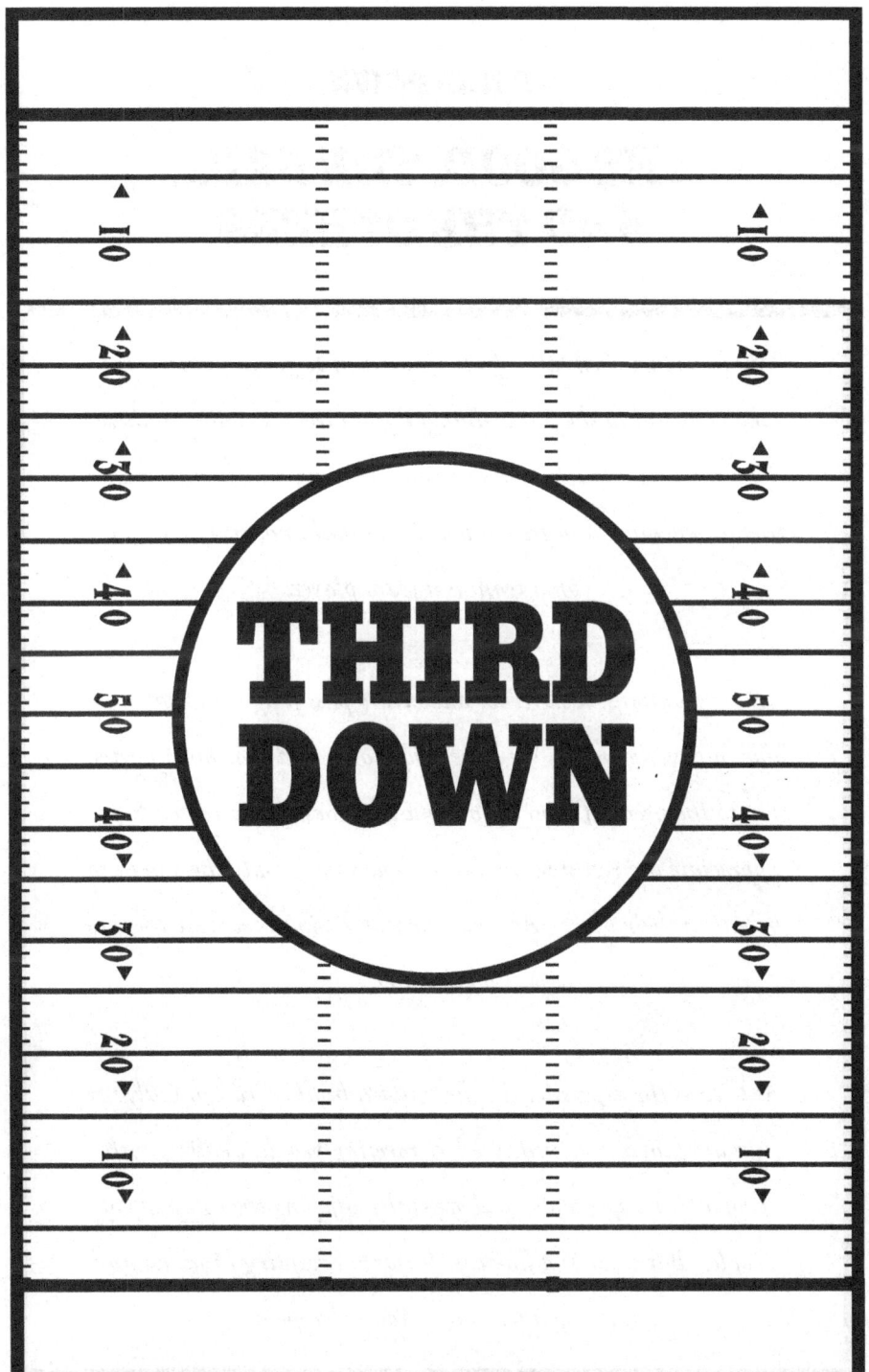

- THIRD DOWN -
THE GOOD, THE BAD...
AND THE OTHERS

We have met them all—from gentlemen to gentle giants, from the powerful to the power-hungry, from the wannabes to those who can't get enough, and everyone in between. We have made friends, enemies, and frenemies. News flash: not everyone who is on a team is a team player.

In our positions, we are not allowed to pass judgment, not even able to pass the buck. We have a job to do and that means catering to the needs of those who are used to being catered to. Some appreciate the gestures, no matter how small, and others need to be put in their place. And on several occasions, we were there to do that too.

As trite as the expression is, the Ballard brothers can proudly say we are people-oriented. We like meeting people, dealing with people, helping people, and generally enjoying the company of people. But there is a fine line between accepting kindness and taking advantage. Yes, it happens.

THEY SIGN YOUR CHECKS!

They sign your checks…no not the owners, not the management…the fans. Without the fans, there would be no game. So, I tend to think of the fans as much a part of the game as the players and team organizations themselves. It is always reassuring to see when the players step up and recognize the fans in a special way. Similarly, not every player plays the game and, to me, is not part of the game.

Quarteback Jim Kelly was with the Buffalo Bills for eleven seasons and when he came to play in Chicago, we Bears had kind of slumped into irrelevancy while the Bills were riding high. You knew when you came to Chicago, you would get a good game out of the Bears, but it would inevitably be a win for the visitors. So, imagine everyone's surprise on this Sunday when the Bears beat the Bills. Not just beat them but beat them up. It didn't sit well with Jim Kelly.

When Kelly came out of the locker room, he looked defeated. His mind was somewhere else, and he cast his head down. In my mind, he was not going to want to face the gauntlet of fans that lined the barriers on the way to the team buses. Normally, as I escorted the visitors to their respective buses, they would stop along the way to sign autographs or simply say hello to the waiting fans. Not today. Not for Kelly.

I asked him if he was okay and if he would want to stop and sign. He was a big guy, about 6'3", so to see him dejected and slumped was enough of an answer. He just shook his head no.

The fans don't know from emotions, and they called out and pushed their mini helmets and paraphernalia out for signing. Kelly walked on by with me at his side between the barrier and bruiser. He got onto the bus and just sat in one of the front seats. The fans, still able to see him through the windows, called out for him. Eventually, he looked up.

There at the end of the row of fans was a girl in a wheelchair. Clearly, she wasn't injured but rather wheelchair-bound. She had a helmet in her lap and just sat quietly looking up at the bus. Something clicked for Jim Kelly when he saw her. He got up, filling the frame of the bus doorway, looked at me, then at her, and walked over to her. She lit up. He signed her helmet and spent a few moments with her.

He patted her on the head and looked down the gauntlet. I asked him if he was okay and he nodded yes. He proceeded to walk the fan line, signing whatever he could until it was time to leave. It was emotional to see his transformation in understanding where the heart of the game really lies. It wasn't about him. It was all about them. He had a bad day…but he made that girl's day…and that made my day.

--Tom

It was New Year's Eve and a nightmare of a schedule! You see we were on a flex game schedule, whereby the television network could literally change the start time of the game to fit their needs. We were playing the Green Bay Packers and were a 3 pm kickoff. Remember this was New Year's Eve and people had plans for the evening, so flexing us out to a later time would be disastrous for ticket holders. But that is just what happened. With the later start time, the game was going to creep well into the evening hours to 7 o'clock and, as people opted out of coming to see us in favor of their celebration plans, inevitably many tickets suddenly became available.

I get a call. It seems my next-door neighbor's son was able to get tickets now for the later game. He is a veteran, and the call was to see if there was anything I could do to make his and his wife's visit special. I make no promises but take his number and begin to wonder what I can do. I want to do something, not just because he is a veteran but because of why he is retired. He was wounded in action—shot in the temple. It was a horrific incident and a heroic event that deserves everything I can do to make his visit to the ironically named Soldier Field memorable.

In the meantime, I have a job to do. I see that Deanna Favre, Brett's wife, has arrived. We exchange pleasantries as I escort her to her box and wish her a happy New Year.

I text the kid at halftime and let him know I have secured wristbands for him and his wife which will get him into Bears Alley after the game as if he were the player's family members. But I must get them to him.

So, I meet up with him and his wife. He has a noticeable scar on his temple and rather thick glasses as a result of his injury. It reminds me of why I am doing what I am doing. I tell him to wait at gate 13 after the game and I will come get him and escort him down. I tell him not to move until I get there.

"I will bring you over to the Packer's side because I work on the visitor's side," I explain to him.

My plan was that as soon as I get the coaches in place after the game, I would come back to get the kid and bring him back. But you know what they say about the best-laid plans?

After the game, I get a call that Deanna wants to come down to the locker room and needs an escort and that means I most likely will not be able to get the kid. I fear this is going to be a bust. I was already feeling terrible. But the game isn't over yet. There still might be time, if I time this right.

I meet Deanna and she is stopping to take pictures and sign autographs every step of the way, slowing down the process of getting her to the locker room. There are still a few minutes left in the game. I get her into the room and then the press starts in. Interviews and pictures. And I am simply waiting. I have yet to get the coaches settled. By the time I finish my duties, the stadium is empty, and I feel terrible. There are just loose hot dog wrappers flying across the field. It was this poor guy's one shot and I let him down. He is not at the designated spot.

Just as I turned the final corner to make my way back, I catch out of the side of my eye, the veteran and his wife standing there—not where I told him to be, but good enough.

"Come on, let's go."

We get into a golf cart and go flying around the field to the visitor's side. Once inside the locker area, I see Deanna but not Brett. I walked over to her and explained his story and asked her if she would please come over and meet the couple. She comes over and is delightful, taking pictures, signing programs, and making small talk.

For some reason, it is a madhouse in the locker room. I signaled to the equipment manager that if he saw Favre come out from the other room to signal me and I would try to bring him over. My equipment friend, Red, wished me good luck as it was a media frenzy going on.

What we didn't know was Favre was in the back at the podium announcing his retirement.

Within a short amount of time, Deanna was pulled away to join Brett in the other room. When the door opens to let her in, there is a blinding strafing of camera flashes. Again, I am confused by the hoopla.

The couple and I were left standing to wait. Maybe five minutes go by and the door opens again and we get the signal to come in. We stay cautiously in the background. The media has gone, and security is all around. I felt that just seeing Brett Favre may have been a memory enough for the couple. It was already 11:30 pm on New Year's Eve, on a fateful day for the man. He didn't need us bothering him now. But, yet again Deanna stepped up and waved us over.

"I want you to meet two of my friends," she said to Brett.

The wife just happened to be wearing a Favre jersey which he immediately appreciated and signed. As if he's known them all his life, he says to them, "You know it's snowing up in Appleton." That was where they were from. (He was cued from the conversation Deanna had with them earlier. But only a gentleman would make the reference.). Even I was impressed. I thought they were going to faint. Without prompting, he asked if they would like a picture. I think you can imagine the answer.

It seemed as if Brett would have stayed but security wanted to usher him along. Things ended quickly after the picture-taking. It seemed right that on that night when a career was ending, and a new year was beginning that one dream came true. Tears literally welled in their eyes for what he had done and how he made them feel. On that night, of all nights, when it was all about him, he made time to make it about them.

That's when you know, it is a career well spent. Because from my perspective, from where I stood that evening, from my tear-filled eye, the fan made the man.

--Tom

When it comes to the military, the key players seem to have a special place in their hearts. And it is heartwarming to see. I can't help but remember one special afternoon in the early 2000s when hardcore military men turned into ten-year-old boys in the face of a football hero. And the football hero gushed at America's real heroes.

Flyovers were a moment to behold. They were held to honor the military when the NFL honors the armed forces. We had our share of Air Force flyovers over the years, and I never stopped being impressed or respectful of what they represented.

It was traditional when there was a flyover, the pilots attended the game if they could and then got to stand afterward in the Alley for a meet and greet with the players.

At the time the Bears were playing the Indianapolis Colts and, of course, the star quarterback at the time was Peyton Manning. When the game was over, everyone was waiting for the big guy to come out of the locker room so they could catch a glimpse.

I could see the pilots were nervous which surprised me. They were fighter pilots, after all. Facing combat missions and precise air maneuvering, nothing should scare them—certainly not a brush with a celebrity.

But they stood there fidgeting, unsure and uncomfortable in their own skins.

Players came out but nothing struck them like the emergence of Manning. He is a big guy, all of 6'5', and has what I would call that Hollywood "IT" factor—a magnetism, a charisma—that tells you he commands the room. They stood in awe. No one said a word.

Manning walks right up to them. "Hey fellas," he begins, "I really appreciate what you guys have done and what you guys continue to do for us."

They didn't know what to say. They shook hands with mutual admiration, but it was obvious he had reduced these badass airmen to little boys.

"Do you want to get a picture?"

99% of the time, I would have approached the player ahead of time and made sure they were okay with the goings-on, but Manning was clearly in command and even seemed to be enjoying entertaining these guys. At one point, he did look over to me and with a wink indicated that he was all good.

The whole experience took me back to when I was a kid when I met my first professional sports player, Luis Aparicio who played for the White Sox. He was Venezuelan and exotic. I was just a kid, but I was in awe. You don't get that feeling out of your mind, ever, that you are in the presence of greatness. I can see that same expression on the faces of the airman with Manning and knew right then that this was life-changing for them.

I can't help but wonder what it means to the player. They meet so many fans, but it was clear on this day that Manning was a fan of the men he was meeting. There was a mutual appreciation for the job well done. Does that change the player? Make him a little more humble about the position he holds. It would be nice to think that Bears Alley is a two-way street!

--Tom

Sometimes it's the little gestures that make the biggest impact.

We were at old Soldier Field in the mid-90s playing Cincinnati not long before Boomer Esiason retired. We were down on the field doing warm-ups long before the game. John Madden had come down to have a chat with Boomer. Back in those days, the fans had easy access to the field, so I was posted to make sure no one rushed the players or, in this case, Madden.

Boomer was tossing the ball around with the other players, talking to Madden. By now, several announcers had made their way to the field for informal pre-game "chats" with the players. It was nothing out of the ordinary.

When the players were done and made their way back to and through the tunnel, many times the local kids would hang over the sides looking for autographs. That too was nothing out of the ordinary.

Autographs in those days were not what they have become today. The kids were not armed with memorabilia or paraphernalia to have signed. Back then, they may just have a piece of paper or such—no jerseys, helmets, footballs, pictures, or collectibles.

So, Boomer finishes with Madden and walks toward the Alley with a ball clutched under his arm. At the bottom of the Alley stood two brothers, nothing in hand, frankly, looking a little sad.

They started calling out "Boomer! Boomer!"

There was just something about them. They caught my attention. They caught Esiason's as well. He tossed them the ball.

Now, ordinarily, they were obligated to give the ball back. Clearly, Boomer wanted them to have it. "There you go boys," he said as he ran off.

They lit up and ran up the bleachers to who appeared to be a waiting father.

I know it is just a little gesture. But to see their faces and to know that moment changed their lives meant everything. What does it take to change a life…the smallest of gestures.

There are small gestures and then there are small people.

I know it firsthand, and I have seen it in action in a player named Emmitt Smith.

I can't take away Smith's accomplishments. He is, after all, the league's all-time leading rusher—breaking the Bears' Walter Payton's record. Yes, he is in the Football Hall of Fame and the College Football Hall of Fame. There are those three Super Bowl rings. Kudos for that. Clearly, humility didn't come with any of it.

I was always a bit of a photo buff and tried when all possible to catch some candid moments of the players for my own personal collection. Well, it just so happens, that during one game back at old Soldier Field, when Smith was still with the Cowboys, I got a great shot of him running out of Bears Alley…a pretty good one, in fact - good enough, that I had it printed up as an 8 x 10.

I put it in my collection and didn't think much more about it until the beginning of the 2000s when I see the Bears schedule come out and I saw that we were going to be playing the Arizona Cardinals—the team Smith had been traded to now in the fading end of his career. With the game day approaching, I pulled out the picture and saw an opportunity.

The game was unremarkable except for the fact that the Cardinals were stranded in Chicago afterward. There was a problem with the pilot of their plane, and they needed to wait for several hours for a replacement pilot to be found. I thought this layover would be a perfect opportunity to approach Smith.

"Mr. Smith," I began and introduced myself. "I took this picture here at the stadium when you were with the Cowboys, and I was wondering if you would mind signing it for me."

He took the picture, took one look at it, and without speaking, handed it back to me and walked away. Not a word was spoken.

Across the way was a grouping of several Bears family members who too asked for autographs. They also got the same treatment.

It was beyond rude. It is one thing to not want to sign an autograph but to silently snub the asker is just…well…unnecessary.

Just as I was licking my wounds the public relations man for the Cardinals approached me and mentioned that he saw what happened. He asked to see the picture.

"He wasn't going to sign your picture because it doesn't have a hologram on it," he explained. "The hologram means you purchased the picture with his endorsement and that he would get a percentage of the purchase price."

"I took this picture," I countered.

"He doesn't sign anything." The inference was clear. He was going to make a profit from my picture. So why bother?

As I said earlier, a simple gesture can make all the difference. Both did. One was based on kindness and respect. The other is based on greed. But I can assure you, both make a difference.

--Tom

HOLIER THAN THOU... CAN I GET AN AMEN?

Separation of church and state is the concept the Republic of the United States is built upon. For some in the NFL, it seems there is no separation between spirituality and the game. You don't "get game" without going with God.

Tim Tebow taking a knee. It's a thing. It is called "Tebowing" and it is a reflection of his deep, deep faith. Many have said that he would take a knee during the National Anthem. To that allegation, he has responded with a declarative "No!" He believed in standing tall for the country. Kneeling during the National Anthem was all a Colin Kaepernick controversy. No, what Tebow is known for is taking a knee and offering up a prayer before and after every game to his Lord. It's unabashed and on the record. Even the Associated Press made note of it when he was playing opposite the Bears on December 11th, 2011, playing against the Denver Broncos in Denver, when Tebow knelt to say his prayers in the end zone.

This all started when he was in high school and carried on through his short-lived professional career. A short career? Perhaps the man above had a different divine plan for young Tebow…but that is a conversation between the two of them.

He took his religion very seriously, going so far as to place scripture on the black underlining below his eyes. His defense of the action was more of a rationalization: "I was just putting on my eye black and I realized that if I put a Bible verse on it, somebody might actually get something out of it," Tebow said back in the day. "It's just gained more and more momentum and steam, more and more people have recognized it, and now it's just got a life of its own."

Reportedly he was even a virgin before he got married. But he comes by his faith honestly. His parents were Baptist missionaries in the Philippines in the 1980s.

But being too nice was just too much for most colleagues. He was a polarizing figure. You either loved him or hated him. But the fans seemed to love him…a least the Christian folk. Thousands would flock to autograph signings. Every autograph was a chance to spread the word. He often signed his name along with GB2—meaning God Bless and Go Broncos. And God bless him for charging a minimum of $160-250 per autograph. Didn't Jesus cast out the moneymakers…or something like that? Didn't Judas cash Jesus in for a pittance in silver? I don't want to get in the way of free commerce and stop the guy from making an almighty buck…but should he be cashing in on the Almighty? I'm just asking WWJD: What would Jesus do? (Allegedly and to his defense, Tebow tithes a healthy amount of his earnings to his Christian charities and is well known for his association with A NIGHT TO SHINE through which his Tim Tebow Foundation aligns 642 churches in 46 countries to create a prom night for special needs children.)

Tebow wasn't the first and probably wouldn't be the last to evoke the Lord to make 'it" work during a game. I happened to be standing on the field when the great announcer/sportscaster Pat Summerall was talking to Troy Aikman. Aikman, who himself went on to be a distinguished sportscaster, was then the quarterback for the Dallas Cowboys. He wasn't playing this game as he was on the injured list but was just running the stairs, joining the warm-up for some exercise. I stood guard, so the fans who could have easily had access to the field didn't get access to Aikman. Summerall with his waft of gray hair and his distinguished voice, walked the field with the "boys" to get a little colorful one-on-one time. Apropos of nothing, the conversation with Aikman turns into an anecdote about Reggie White.

It wasn't so much WWJD but rather what would Reggie White do? White was known as the Minister of Defense because, despite being one of the most awarded defensive ends in the NFL, playing for the Philadelphia Eagles, Green Bay Packers, and Carolina Panthers, he was also an ordained evangelical minister. Unlike Tebow, White had the respect of his peers for his religious pursuits and beliefs. It was no joke.

Summerall went on to talk about the time when White was playing for the Packers he was lined up against a rookie who was all full of piss and vinegar—thinking he could take the legend down on the line. The rookie was told that the best way to get White down was to get under his skin. So, as they lined up, the kid tries to bust White's stones—talking crap about him. He makes some derogatory remarks about his mother. Hike! The kid is tackled with little to no mercy. They line again. The kid tries his next best shot. Same result. As they line up for the third time, White takes the initiative: "Jesus is coming," he says to the kid. "And you're not ready." Hike!

You can imagine what happened after that.

Summerall let out an almighty laugh, anecdote over.

I have noticed a lot of players on the field wearing their Jesus on the cross. Plenty of players acknowledge the heavens above after a touchdown. But I don't know how much clout the New Orleans Saints have with the big guy above as they have only won one Superbowl (2010) since the franchise began in 1967. What's the point of being a "Saint" if God's guys don't have the edge? Full disclosure, I am a practicing Christian. But even I am not sure there is room for God on the gridiron. Just like I don't believe there is room for politics, racism, homophobia, or any other polarizing subject matter. (Take note Colin Kaepernick and the next one like him.) It is not whether Tim Tebow should not have his beliefs. He is certainly allowed. But is the playing field a place to make a statement or should it be a neutral territory? Too much of a "good" thing…is just too much.

So, let's have God sit on the sidelines with Chet and me. We will surely get him into Bears Alley with V.I.P. status should he show up for a one-on-one with any player. Until then everyone is free to have their beliefs. But let's not believe anyone is holier than thou.

Because, clearly, the Lord works in mysterious ways…for all of us.

--Tom

PASSING THE BUCK!

Money! It is such a touchy subject. I have found it has never stopped making people look foolish—whether giving or receiving. No matter how much is in play, there is no simple way to pass the buck...

I earned, or at least inherited, my chops from George Mandich. It always amazed me that as an FBI agent he didn't tweak to the realization that he was putting all this responsibility in the hands of just a boy in his teens. Early on, he would walk me into the coaches' locker room and say, "I'm George Mandich, the head of NFL security in Chicago. Here is my guy, Chet. He is going to walk you coaches up to the box. Can you just touch base with him right here so we can figure out whatever you need?"

Over time I didn't need the introduction but early on it gave me the validity I required. Hell, I was a kid, and these coaches were leaders of men. Mandich's mandate clearly stuck with some of the coaches from the get-go...I was his man.

On Christmas Eve in 1994, and we could call that later on in my tenure, the Bears were playing the New England Patriots and Bill Parcells was the coach at the time. (I know everyone thinks of that other Bill… Belichick…as the only "Bill" associated with the Patriots, but we are going back some days here.) Parcells walks out dressed to the "nines" in a beautifully tailored suit and starts with, "Where's Chet?"

I'm not sure if the call was for the good or the bad—had I done something wrong, or did he need something done?

"I am right here," I state, standing somewhat at attention.

He pulls out a bankroll of hundred-dollar bills and peels one off to hand to me.

"I am sorry Mr. Parcells, but I can't take that."

Tips were strictly forbidden and as much as I wanted…needed… the money, I couldn't. He tries to jam it into my hand.

"God Dammit! It's Christmas Eve. Take the hundred dollars," he demanded and pressed the note into my chest. There was little I could do. This was a standoff. As much as he was making a kind gesture, he was clearly getting angry at the insolent newbie turning down his generosity. He was looking like a fool, and I was the one doing it to him. I blinked and took the money appreciatively.

It didn't have to get to that. What is wrong with a holiday gift for a presumed job well done? Why shouldn't I be able to graciously accept what was offered to me? It may not seem to be, but it really was a conundrum. I know my job forbids tips but was it really in my job description to piss off the visiting coach? Would we be having the same conversation if he had offered me a box of candy, a necktie, or a winter scarf? I didn't think so.

To be honest it felt like dirty money at this point. His gesture had turned into a mandate—not given out of generosity but rather out of stubborn arrogance. He was no longer respecting my parameters but buying my appreciation toward him.

Still, it was Christmas Eve. He got what he wanted, and I got what I deserved. Win/win. The misunderstanding may have lingered…but the buck stopped there.

--Chet

Tyrone Keys was one of the "Shuffling Crew"—those Super Bowl-winning teammates who put together that now infamous music video after the big win for the Bears. He is also what was considered in days gone by financially illiterate—something that was very prevalent with hot young, well-paid, athletes back in the day who came into good money too fast and were never educated on what to do with it.

One of my pals in the organization made a few bucks—what we now would call a side hustle—washing the players' cars over in the Halas Hall garage. There was nothing particularly interesting about that. But word spread fast that he was good, and soon everyone wanted their car done by him, including Tyrone Keys.

No problem with the wash. The problem was getting paid.

Tyrone asked if he could pay with a check.

"Fine," my pal informed him.

This is where the problem started. Tyrone had no idea how to fill out a check.

"Do you mind if I just hand you the checkbook," he began. "Just fill it out with what you need, and I will sign it."

Now, a more unscrupulous man could have seen this as an opportunity. Fortunately, that is not what my friend was about. Yet, I couldn't help but wonder how many others weren't so honest in Key's life. Had he been swindled or taken over the years and for how much? You hear these stories of pro athletes losing it all and wonder how that can be. Clearly, it can start with a car wash and the car isn't getting cleaned…they're getting cleaned out.

--Chet

Barry Sanders was on the hurt list…but, from my perspective, nothing hurt more than his wallet. I found that out in the coaches' box during a Detroit Lions game.

Most of the coaches no longer allowed me to sit up in the coaches' box but for some reason, the Detroit Lions had no problem with it. So, I looked forward to the Bears playing the Lions. It gave me somewhere to be once the game began. Sanders, being on the hurt list, opted to sit out the game with coaches in the booth as well. He seemed to be an affable enough guy, not that I was going to have any real conversation with him…or so I thought.

For my acceptance into the booth, I chose to play host and asked everyone if they needed anything. The coaches' box was always catered with hot dogs and soft drinks, that sort of thing, and the guys generally opted to take advantage of those goodies. My asking if anyone needed anything was more of an empty gesture. It simply made me look valued in the room. Sanders didn't get the ruse. He pipes up with, "I'll have a hot chocolate," as if he was ordering off a menu.

He wasn't demanding or a diva about the request, it was just that hot chocolate wasn't readily available. Did he really think I was the cater waiter for the box? I would have to go down to the concession stand on the lower level and wait in line with the throngs of others, pay for the drink, and bring it back—presuming it would even be hot by the time the process was over.

I did the obligatory 'hemming' and 'hawing' discreetly, trying to indicate that, yes, this drink would have to be paid for…and I should not be the one, the lowest on the totem pole, to do so. I stood there for a minute or two and waited to see if he was going to put his hand in his pocket. He didn't. I figured I would pay with my money, and he would pay me back when I got back.

It took me some time, for this mission of mercy. I had hoped that my uniform would have garnered me some clout with the vendor, but it didn't. I waited in line with the rest of the hoi polloi and, with chocolate in hand and dollars less in my wallet, made my way back.

Once back, I handed the lukewarm chocolate to Sanders. Nothing. No "thank you." No money—let alone a reimbursement but, heaven forbid, a tip. Again, nothing.

That put two of us on the hurt list.

Needless to say, I didn't ask him if he needed anything else. I often wonder if I should have just handed him the receipt and waited there with all the expectation of getting paid that he had of getting his hot chocolate.

Being an Andy Frain meant catering to every need. I just didn't expect it to be at my "expense"…literally.

--Chet

JUST ONE OF THE GUYS... UNTIL YOU'RE NOT!

Cam Newton has a reputation…and everyone who knows him says he lives up to it. He had balls and I don't mean footballs. The problem was Newton seemed to live in his world, which was very big compared to the world around him. And that is far from conducive to making friends and influencing people. When you are a quarterback, the team, the fans, and the media expect you to be a guiding light, not to just absorb the spotlight and when things go wrong dim the light. Cam Newton may just need to see the light.

You can't take his attributes away from Newton. He came out of the gate at a full gallop, being named Offensive Rookie of the Year. He holds the record for being the league's first rookie to throw for 4000 yards in his first season and the first to throw for 400 yards in an NFL debut. The guy's got game. No doubt. He just doesn't have gamesmanship.

Being gracious is part of being a player—win or lose. Cam may have skipped that etiquette lesson in favor of being a more sullen loser who could only be perceived as a sore loser. Take his walking out of his mono-syllabic press conference after his leading the Carolina Panthers to a Superbowl loss against the Denver Broncos in 2016. He was sacked six times, the most in Superbowl history. Instead of taking it like a man or even taking one for the team, he took it hard and made it personal. But that brands the team, not just the player, and if you are going to be a leader…then lead.

The next day, after his walkout, he faced the cameras yet again to explain away his rude behavior as an overwhelmingly emotional moment. He informed everyone that he had no regrets, stating that he simply didn't want to talk to the media—as is the traditional quarterback role to fulfill, post-game. He proceeded to explain that he still did not want to talk to the media but he did with such pithy insights as: "I am who I am…and I don't have to conform to anyone else's wants…I am not that guy…I've been on record as saying I am a sore loser. Who wants to lose? Show me a good loser and I will show you a loser." He went on to extoll that he was his own person and that he was fine with that and took pride in it. He also claimed that he never once offended anybody. Now that could be debated.

I saw his antics firsthand, again after a loss—this time to the Bears. I hadn't really been paying attention to the post-game activities other than making sure the Panthers were all set on the buses to depart.

I made one last sweep of the locker room to make sure I could give the okay for the filled buses to leave the stadium. It was almost sixty minutes after the game, so the timing was right, and everything seemed on schedule. When I walked in, the room seemed all clear. And then I heard it. A shower was turned on.

Out of my peripheral vision, I see a man sitting on the bench.

"What's going on?" I asked innocently enough.

"Cam," is all he could muster, and shrugged his shoulders.

"What are you talking about?" I couldn't believe what I was hearing. "The entire team…the players, the coaches, everyone is on the buses waiting to leave. Is he just getting in the shower now?"

Again, a shrug of the shoulders was all he could respond. It was Cam being Cam. It's his world and the rest of the team just lives in it.

Believe me, the last thing I wanted to do was to face the coaches who would have to explain to the rest of the team on the buses that they had to wait for Cam to get out of the shower, but that was exactly what I had to do. You can imagine the reaction.

About half an hour later, he emerged unapologetic. He took his place on the bus and the buses left. And so did my respect.

Taking into account the laws of physics, what goes up, must come down. Newton found himself on the outside looking in, bounced from a highly anticipated start with the New England Patriots post-Brady and a disastrous return to the Panthers.

Now living the life of a free agent, he might be out there pedaling his mad skills. But does anyone want to work with somebody who is just perpetually maddening?

My experience with Cam left me wondering just how today's big names would be to deal with. Would it be equally as disappointing, or would I be in for some surprises? I had dealt with big names and big egos before—for the good or bad of the experience—but these days are different: big money, fractured teams, and superstardom are all at play. Not to mention social media only magnifies a person's reputation, whether it is deserved or not.

If you want to chalk up a surprise, that must be Bill Belichick, the seemingly gruff and cantankerous head coach of the New England Patriots. From the sideline to the media conference, Belichick doesn't seem to crack a smile—a curmudgeon of a coach. Everything about him says: keep your distance. Sorry to ruin a reputation here, but that may just be an act for the cameras.

The Belichick I have seen is more Jekyll than Hyde. (For the record, Hyde was the bad guy in that split personality.) The Belichick I have seen and met cracked jokes. That's right, the guy's got a sense of humor. And clearly, the joke was on me.

Belichick's guy at the time was equally affable. Tom Brady. The GOAT: Greatest Of All Time! Pin-up perfect. He seemingly has it all, which means every reason to love him is every reason to hate him…except you can't. He's just so damn nice.

If there ever was a player I would have given a pass to for having earned the right to be someone standoffish, aloof, or distant, it would have been Brady. But no. His "aw shucks" politeness and approachability made me think he was from television's fictional Mayberry of Andy Griffith fame.

I had met him a couple of times, but I have to confess, that unlike meeting the dozens—make that hundreds—of players, I met over my tenure, there is just something about being in the presence of greatness that is a bit humbling. I say humbling but not paralyzing and like a good Ballard brother I didn't want to miss the opportunity for an autograph. So, I obligatorily bought a 'just-in-case' jersey.

The Patriots trounced the Bears that day, the GOAT on perfect form. I had invited my son Tommy to the game and subsequently down to Bears Alley afterward. Tom, not surprisingly, had media obligations after the game. I stood and watched as Tom was passed from one media outlet to the next, always greeting them like they were old friends rather than a necessary evil.

Then came my moment. He was between interviews and just standing there looking around. I walked up and pointed out Tommy to him and then asked if he would mind signing a jersey for him. He couldn't have been nicer with the request and signed it on the shoulder.

I immediately flashed back to my moment with Emmitt Smith who wouldn't sign my photo or autographs for the fans because I and they weren't sporting "authorized" memorabilia for which he got a monetary cut of the action.

Tom could have easily brushed me aside under the guise of all that was going on around him. Nor did he push aside a number of fans afterward who surrounded him and asked for autographs and pictures as he made his way to the players' bus. Are we not sure the "G" in GOAT doesn't stand for "Gentleman?"

I hope that rubs off on the next generation coming up. Certainly, the next great hope is Patrick Mahomes, the half-a-billion-dollar contracted quarterback to the Kansas City Chiefs. With that kind of money on the line, you know there is an expectation that he is the next Brady…or better. But as we have seen before, money corrupts, alienates, segregates, and…well…changes a person, those who are willing to be changed. Too young. Too much. Too soon. That is what people were saying about Mahomes. There is no way this rookie would be able to have perspective and keep his feet on the ground.

I was expecting the worst when he and his family arrived. He could have been a real ass about the fact that the Bears had overlooked him during the draft. But that was water under the bridge and a lucrative contract ago. His brother already had a reputation for being "out of control" in whatever form that was taking and Mahomes, himself, was being pulled in a million directions and none of them were pulling him to the field to play. I stepped in.

"Is there anything I can do?" I asked.

"Please just make sure my family is taken care of," he instructed… not as a diva directive, but rather out of genuine concern the Mahomes name seemed to generate.

I stood for a moment and took it all in. Here was this kid, in just his early 20s, whose life overnight had altered greatly and was expected to do his job with elevated expectations while managing the circus-like chaos that surrounds his insta-fame. And he was handling it like a pro. No attitude. No pushback. No kidding. A GOAT in the making? Only if the "G" in "Greatest" stands for on-field…and off.

It does seem that quarterbacks attract the most attention and rightfully so. They are the focal point of the game, for the most part, and the leaders of the team. Still, there was one who couldn't wait to ask us guys about what's fun to do in the city and what was our favorite deep-dish pizza—a Chicago institution which he found intriguing—and just have an ordinary conversation about…well… ordinary things. He got away with it because, unlike other quarterbacks who passed through Bears Alley, he wasn't swamped by fans or overwhelmed with requests. He was just Eli Manning of the New York Giants, who, in my opinion, had probably gotten used to being 'just' Eli Manning. He did, after all, live in the shadow of his older, more standout brother, Peyton Manning, of the Indianapolis Colts fame and later still, the Denver Broncos.

Now it is hard to call Eli the less successful brother. Both are two-time Superbowl champions and it is Eli who was the two-time Superbowl MVP to Peyton's one selection. Still, it seems that Peyton had more spotlight, more presence, and more of "IT" than Eli which made Eli totally accessible during the conversations we had. He was just one of us guys.

There is an old British expression that comically defines their two popular American football derivative national sports: soccer and rugby. Soccer, it is said, is played by gentlemen and enjoyed by thugs, and rugby is played by thugs and enjoyed by gentlemen. I wonder where that adage stands back across the pond with our football. The Cam Newtons of the game set one standard while so many others set a…dare I say it…higher standard.

You can't hint at disrespect until you have earned everyone's respect. There are plenty who need to learn that to be a better player you have to be a better man. If you want to be just one of the boys…be a man. What will it take for American football to be universally played by gentlemen? I am just asking for the British.

--Tom

Game over. Time to let loose. We never got the chance to tailgate as we had to be on-site and ready to go long before the start of the game. It all started with a few beers in the employee parking lot where between beers we would pitch golf balls back into the stadium. For the record, I had a pretty good swing. Over time things escalated and soon we were letting our hair down, underground. It was a buffet in the players' parking garage each Sunday.

This was as open an event as there was. As we've described, everyone was invited—from the Andy Frain folk to the players who were on their way to their cars. Food was always plentiful as we got most of what was left over from the coaches' and V.I.P. boxes sent down to us. The guy who oversaw catering of the skyboxes, Wojo, knew of our little endeavor and always ordered extra, so we would have enough of the good stuff. And of course, people such as friends, wives, and girlfriends would make things each week—it was all very potluck. We, in turn, would deliver any leftover food down to the homeless on Wacker Drive.

Ours was a popular pit stop and on average 25-30 , sometimes as many as 40, people would hang out—not to mention those who would just pass through. Steve McMichael and his beautiful wife, Debra Marshall, who was the "IT" couple of the team, were frequent fliers at our little soiree and that gave it status. Not long after, the multi-million-dollar players were swapping beers with us, lowly day players.

The garage itself was underground, a dank place really, but it was good for protecting us from the uncertain Chicago weather. There was no ventilation and really had only one way out. I tell you this because one Sunday, Tom Greenfield—a long-time employee—brought his much-talked-about venison as a special treat. We got the clever idea of barbequing up the meat right there and then.

Out came a portable Weber, some coals, and the requisite lighter fluid and we were in business. Once a good flame was going, the slabs of meat were thrown on the grill. Within minutes, the flames flared, and the smoke billowed…and billowed. The problem was, there was nowhere for the smoke to vent out. It just kept billowing and before long, you could not see your hand in front of you for the venison fog. Among those we were choking out were defensive lineman Dan Hampton and placekicker Kevin Butler. It was never wise to asphyxiate the star players.

Those players who were still in the locker room were furious as they could not get to their cars as there was nothing to do to dissipate the smoke. It was a disaster and all we could do was stand around and "rearrange the furniture on the Titanic." Eventually…and I can say it took some time…the smoke cleared, and the venison idea turned to "Oh dear." The administration got involved.

They couldn't exactly say we put the building in danger, as the garage was a virtual cement bunker but, nonetheless, they weren't pleased. They claimed they had no idea that these post-game parties were a thing—although, I still believe they had to have known all along and just turned a blind eye—and hooked us with not being allowed to continue them… at least in the garage.

The players made it known that we were morons for having pulled such a stunt—despite having participated on more than one Sunday. You have to love hypocrisy when shit hits the fan…or in this case, venison hits the grill. But the worst of it was because of those moments we were bonded, part of the team. Until it all went up in smoke…literally. They had made us feel like just one of the guys…that is…until you're not.

--Chet

BEHIND EVERY GREAT MAN... AND THEY DESERVE WHAT THEY GET!

She got in the elevator and stood with his brother who was always cool with me and whom I liked a lot and his devoted mother who would make the trek as often as possible to catch a game, and was someone, again, whom I really liked.

"I'm here to see Brian Urlacher," she declared. "How do I get to and into the locker room?"

There was a moment of silence among everyone else on the elevator. Was she serious? I shot her that look, a look of amazement, that clearly said: "Are you crazy?"

It was halftime and, yes, the players were in the locker room but what was she thinking? Did she think they were just sitting around waiting for friends and family to pop in for a visit? That is, given she fits either of those criteria.

"I'm afraid visitors are not allowed in the locker room," I stammered, still stunned by my ongoing disbelief at her request.

"It's okay," she continued, oblivious. "I'm his girlfriend."

That clinched it. She wasn't going anywhere close to the locker room.

Brian Urlacher is a player…or should I say "playa." There is no doubt. He plays the field for sure. But not the gridiron only. Over time, he's played the romance roundup with such notables as Jenny McCarthy. But things didn't always turn out in his favor.

There was that pesky $125 million lawsuit filed by his ex-lover Tyna Robertson, the mother of his son, who claimed that he was spreading false truths that she was responsible for the murder of her late husband who shot and killed himself with her gun during an argument between the two. Nasty stuff. None of that stopped him from playing up his playboy image. And the gals, it seemed, just kept coming.

And one of those gals just happened to be in the elevator with me. The elevator may have gone to the top floor, but I wasn't sure hers did. She seemed, on the kind side, naïve; on the meaner side…a little self-absorbed.

"It doesn't matter who you are," I stated rather emphatically this time, "there are no unauthorized visitors in the locker room."

Fortunately, the elevator reached the designated floor at that point and all parties left for their respective seats. When the doors closed, my co-workers were all giddy and one looked me straight in the eye and with all seriousness asked: "Do you know who that was?"

I shrugged my shoulders.

"Paris Hilton!"

"Oh," I mumbled back. I couldn't believe I didn't recognize her—not that the outcome wouldn't have been the same. Let's face it, who is she really? A reality star who is simply famous for being famous with the catchphrase—"That's Hot!"—a phrase that is no longer in the social zeitgeist. Sorry, sister, it is the locker room lockout for you.

Urlacher wasn't the only player to parade a headline-making bevy of beauties through the stadium. You can't blame the players for being the magnets they are. Let's face it, they are just stunted adolescents who are playing a big game, with big bucks, and swinging a big d*ck. But the wrong woman can only make you look like a d*ck.

You can't just be the "IT" couple. You have to get "it" right—understand there is compromise and collaboration. And some do. Case in point, Seattle Seahawks turned Denver Broncos quarterback Russell Wilson and his wife Ciera.

Wilson led the Seahawks to two Superbowl appearances, winning Superbowl XLVIII and with a goal-line interception losing the next year in Superbowl XLIX. Still, he is Russell Wilson…the man who might not have been. The joke was he had the talent but not the stature when it came time for the college draft. At just 5'10", he was overlooked rather than looked over and fell behind in the choices. Didn't he get the last laugh when in 2019 he signed a $140 million dollar contract—making him the highest-paid player in the NFL at the time?

But what makes him even more powerful is he is one half of a power couple. He is married to pop sensation Cierra—who is successful, beautiful, and, like her husband, knows what it means to be on a team.

I came across them at Soldier Field. After the game, some of the more notable players would ask if we could escort their family members down to a waiting area so that they would have somewhere to stand before the players came out. We got Cierra down without incident and she stood dutifully waiting for Russell by the locker room in Bears Alley. I admired the fact that people approached unabashedly and she, in turn, greeted them all with warm smiles, signed autographs, and took pictures—never complaining that the time was not right, or it was inappropriate. Full disclosure, I got a photo too and she couldn't have been nicer when I approached.

When Russell came out, they kissed, and it was very cute. The public display of affection kind of threw me as Russell is reported to be very religious, signs scripture with his autographs, and that they had been celibate before marriage. What I saw was genuine love.

But what makes them a true "IT" couple is that they understand their role as ambassadors for the game and their craft. Their WHY NOT YOU Foundation raises much-needed dollars for people being lifted out of poverty through education. Russell Wilson understands he is part of a team…on the field and off.

That's the difference between being just a "playa" and a "player". Understanding that what you have been given comes with a responsibility to pay it forward, not play it forward. When I look at Russell Wilson and the others like him, I can only think of the words of Paris Hilton: "That's Hot!"

For the others and we can tell who you are, even if you can't... "That's Not!"

--Tom

Men are pigs. Let's start by stating the obvious. I have said it before. And there are plenty who in public may be gentlemen—and I use that term sparingly—while in private, say the locker room, with the rest of the testosterone tumult, can show a seedier side of their personalities. Sure, there was the teasing of the media women with the dropped towels. Harmless jokes people called it. Sexist harassment others would say. That was relatively nothing. I am talking about the times when anything goes.

My pal in the equipment department was seeing one girl fairly regularly. Now, when we are in the positions we are, there are times you want to impress your gal. My pal thought it would be impressive to allow his girlfriend to bring her friends to the locker room and show them behind-the-scenes after the players had gone. Harmless enough...or so you would think. On this one occasion, my pal's girlfriend brought along a friend who proved to be overly inquisitive.

Before long, the girlfriend's friend disappears along with the long-time equipment staff member. Everyone grows a little concerned until sometime later when back they come through the door leading to the referee's locker room.

"Where the hell did you go?" my friend asks, more out of concern than rebuke. "What the hell were you doing?"

"Wanna smell my fingers?" was all he got in return. Disgusting!

That was the last of my friend's offering of behind-the-scenes anything…I'm not sure if it was the last of the girlfriend as well. But somehow the locker room has this reputation for being a safe place for crossing the line. Like Vegas, what happens here, stays here. I don't ascribe to that notion and fully believe repugnant behavior is intolerable anywhere. But the locker room is like a church, it is a sanctuary. People went to confession all right, but make no mistake, it wasn't a church, and nothing was sacred.

Case in point: Jay Hilgenberg. He got caught with his pants down—having an affair. He wasn't the only one and he wouldn't be the last. But instead of taking his social crime and punishment like a man, he whined like a little bitch and publicly named everyone on the team who also had cheated on their spouse. He busted open the sanctity of the locker room by throwing everyone under the bus. Excommunication for sure. But that still didn't stop the hi-jinx and low living.

What is the point of having a good woman behind you, if you are going behind her? There is a fine line between being the "IT" couple and becoming the "Shit" couple. And I don't blame her. I can't even blame him…completely. I blame the locker room where gang mentality overwhelms common sense. I know they have tried to put an end to college football hazing but as late as 2023 reports have surfaced of naked players dry-humping their freshman newcomers in the locker room showers. How is that a rite of passage? It's not. It is sexual dominance. Dominant on the field, dominant in the bedroom. That's what football instills in these men…and in incubates in the locker room.

Not everyone is guilty of course but I worry that today's mega-millionaire players who've got more game off the field than on, won't learn the lessons of the past and that today's locker room is as toxic to relationships because it is as sexually charged as ever. Players have to start thinking with the right head, in order to keep their head on straight. If these men continue to be pigs, it should only be in that they are bringing home the bacon. Once home, let a good woman show them how to be a real man.

--Chet

It is always a good time when the Longs are on site. They were giants in my eyes. Well, they were giants, period. Dad, the legendary defensive end for the Raiders turned sportscaster Howie Long, towers at 6'5". His son, Bears guard Kyle Long measures in at 6'6" and his older brother, consecutive Superbowl-winning defensive guard, Chris, would be considered the peanut at just 6'3". Yes, there is a Howard Long Jr., who is a football talent scout for the Raiders. He doesn't have to put his body on the line. Good thing. He comes in at just 6' tall. But the one who really stands tall in my eyes is Howie's wife, the boy's mother, Diane.

I had come to know her over time as she would drop in to see Kyle play. Howie, of course, would normally be in the studio doing color commentary at times, and then, at other times, it became a real family affair. Howie, from my perspective, was careful to stand back from the crowds and let Kyle have his day in the sun. Not Diane. She was in the thick of things. Of course, it was easier for her to come and go as she was not the famous face.

When she came to the stadium, I would pick her up in a golf cart and get her to where she needed to go, and along the way, we would chat. She couldn't be nicer. She seemed to care about me as much as I was curious about her famous family. The conversations became a regular thing as I carted her, and sometimes her friends she had visiting, around the stadium.

Diane didn't fall into the category of what people would consider the stereotypical sports spouse. She was arm candy—although a pretty woman with long flowing hair—she was more of a partner who stood beside her husband and not just next to him, because of him.

But speaking of standing next to Howie, I don't know if I would call her petite. Who wouldn't look petite next to her behemoth of a husband? She was a good height for a woman at 5'8" but has an even better head on her shoulders. She studied law, before her days with Howie, but is not a practicing lawyer. She spends her talents watching over the careers of her sons. And for the most part, she flies under the radar.

But not with me. She has that way, a gift really, of making you feel important, relevant, and heard. Not that it seemed at the time that we talked about anything too deep, but she is focused and present. There is a term for it, the professional wife. Jacqueline Kennedy Onassis, Diplomat Pamela Harriman, and Kitty Carlisle are just a few who come to mind and fit that description—complementary additions to powerful or prominent husbands. It is not that they don't have their own interests and careers, but they consider part of that career to be the Mrs. to his Mr. And they work on complimenting the pair as opposed to standing in the limelight. As I said, it isn't arm candy…it's an asset.

Were we friends? She certainly made it seem that way. And that was her way. So, on January 6, 2019, I wanted to return the friendship. It was a big day for the Longs at Soldier Field.

The Philadelphia Eagles were playing the Bears, which meant son Chris would be opposing son Kyle. Diane, of course, was there. And Howie wasn't in the booth but rather in the stands to cheer on both sons. Even Howard Jr. took time from the Raiders to be there. Let's face it, for the Longs, no matter how the game turned out, it was win/win. Although Diane may have shown a little preference by wearing a Bears jersey.

I wanted to make things special for the Longs for all the time Diane made me feel special. First on the agenda was Garrett's popcorn. This popcorn was a Chicago institution gourmet popcorn and not easy to get.

I had the inside track with the company and secured quite a few buckets for the family to share. And from that point on we made sure their needs were catered to as best we could.

For the record, the Bears lost by one point to the Eagles who were the Superbowl champs that year. You could say the eagles were flying high at the time…the Bears hibernating.

My job had me with the visiting team and when the game was over, Diane was right there to congratulate Chris whom she introduced me to the moment he walked out of the locker room. Howie stayed in the background, letting his sons take their moments. I was impressed with how they never let Kyle feel like the loser that day. And when I asked for a picture, Diane was more than pleased…probably even proud…to gather up the family and include me in the shot.

Time has passed and Kyle Long is no longer with the Bears, so I don't see Diane like I used to but that is okay. Because knowing her as I do, I know she is still a mama Bear and taking care of business for the family.

I have met plenty of wives, girlfriends, and significant others to the players on the field. It is as much a job and an obligation as most careers. Trying to maintain your own identity in the shadow of hero worship can't be easy. It takes commitment. And to that end, I have seen some come and I have seen some go. But when it comes to measuring up to the best of them, plenty have a LONG way to go.

--Tom

SEEING RED!

Gordon Batty was his real name. But everyone knew him as "Red." You'd never know it from his now bald head but in his youth, he had a mop of fiery red hair which inspired the nickname. It stuck. And so had he, nearly four decades to the Green Bay Packers as their legendary equipment manager. Despite that longevity, he is probably most famous for helping one player cope with a crushing loss. Not on the field, but in the heart.

Packers' running back, number 33, Aaron Jones, had a particularly close relationship with his father. It was his father, Alvin, who introduced him to football, encouraged him to get into football, attended as many games as he could, and overall, was his biggest supporter. So, when Jones' father died suddenly, the heartbroken player had a medallion made which encased some of his father's ashes so Jones could carry Alvin close to his heart at all times. Touching.

Football is a violent game. And during a game against the Detroit Lions that medallion was ripped off Jones' neck while in the end zone and lost. He was heartbroken. A search was made and the medallion was eventually found by trainer Bryan Engel.

Red saw the dilemma in Jones continuing to wear the medallion during games and came up with his own solution. Of his own accord, Red created a pocket in Jones' jersey, just above his heart—a small pocket, just big enough to hold the medallion and sewn shut before each game so the medallion would stay secure.

That is the kind of guy Gordon "Red" Batty is…a true team player. I tell you that story because Red also stepped up for me, despite not being on the same team.

We had become professional pals over the years as I spent plenty of time in the visitor's locker room and the last person you generally deal with is the equipment manager as he is the last person out the door—having to wrap up the teams' belongings after the players leave. Red couldn't be a nicer guy and as the story above showed, he was willing to do just about anything for anyone…within reason.

I happened to know that Red was also a hockey fan and one day when the Bears played the Packers, Chicago-born Chris Chelios who played hockey for both the Montreal Canadiens and the Detroit Red Wings, and Canada's Brett Hull (son of Hockey legend Bobby Hull) who among others also played for the Red Wings, were both at the game. The two hockey stars didn't have V.I.P. passes or anything to get them down and through Bears Alley but I knew it would mean a great deal to Red to have a chat with the two.

A little finagling, a little negotiating later, and I managed to get a couple of "family passes" and walked them down. Be careful what you ask for. Both had been having what could only be assessed as a "good time." By the time they got to Red, they may have been intoxicated. I'm just speculating.

Nonetheless, Red was thrilled and asked if there was anything he could do for me in return. I told him I would love an autograph from Ahman Green, a Packers running back. Now, as I have mentioned before, I don't get autographs from just any players. They have to be "somebody" in my eyes. Somebody who has proven their worth. And Green had shown his staying power having gone to the Pro Bowl four times while with the Packers. Besides, my son Tommy was crazy about Green as well.

"I'll see what I can do," Red said with no guarantees. I understood.

It was a crazy scene that day and I walked away with no autograph.

I thought little about it. Players are fickle; you have to get them at the right time, in the right frame of mind to even ask for an autograph, so I simply assumed the time was not right or the opportunity had not presented itself. "I'll take care of you later," he promised. But really? Would he? The moment was over.

A year or at least the better part of the next season went by before I saw Red again. He was very excited. "I've got something for you," he said.

He pulled out a pair of used spikes, used by none other than Ahman Green! They were white, with the exception of Ahman's signature.

They were pure gold. I couldn't believe my eyes as Red presented them to me.

"You didn't have to do this," I said, knowing the risk it was to smuggle out equipment like this and then simply give it away.

"We are family," he returned.

Subsequently, we got Aaron Rogers and Clay Matthews to sign the same cleat that Green signed, making it worth thousands on the collector's market—not that I would part with it. It is considered one of my most prized possessions, not only for what it is but for how it came to be. I still, to this day, can't believe the generosity shown to me…especially me being a man from another team. But that is the man Red is. To him, it is not about teamsmanship; it is really about gamesmanship. We are all in this together, not just foes but friends. What do they call it now? Frenemies! As a result, I am one of those guys who is never mad…when seeing Red. And that is what the game is all about!

--Tom

SECOND GENERATION... THE SON ALSO RISES!

I had no problem with the Chicago guys. You'd see them at the games and never think twice. I'm talking about our Chicago homies who would come home despite having made it to the big time: Jim Belushi, Ashton Kutcher, and Vince Vaughn to name a few. Even those who weren't from Chicago but came to support their teams like Keegan Michael Key…a Detroit fan. Yeah, he's been to the stadium. Hell, I could go on. The bottom line, I was never star-struck with those Hollywood types. It was good to see them. Normally, I would leave them to themselves. Except this one time. I couldn't help myself. I just had to approach Vince Vaughn. You see, we have something in common besides the Bears.

Over the years, people…and I mean many people…have told me that I sound just like Vince Vaughn when I speak. Even I have to agree to a certain degree. So, there he was watching the game. I knew he was there. I would just wait for the right moment. Being a huge Bears fan, Vaughn made his way to Bears Alley post-game to hang and wait for the players as the V.I.P.s are prone to do. I hadn't noticed him initially, although that was hard to do at well over six feet tall. My buddies were the ones to point him out to me: "Hey, Tom, there's your guy."

This was my moment. I approached him.

"Hey Vince," I begin, "I just want to let you know that a lot of people say that I sound just like you."

He chuckles. "Really?"

"I have to correct them," I continue. "I let them know that you sound just like me."

With that, he let out an almighty laugh. "So, you're the original."

"Yes sir!"

"Well, it is very nice to meet you," he deferred.

At this point, all my buddies had joined in on the laughter and I asked for a picture—proof, if you will, that I am the "original" and this guy had been ripping off my act for all those years. He was great.

It is clear I have no problem with celebrities. So why, all those years before, did I freeze up? Not just freeze. I downright panicked.

"If you get this autograph for me, I will name my firstborn after you," I begged my brother Chet. Name my first-born after my brother? What was I thinking? What was I promising? Okay, that may have been a bit of hyperbole, but I was desperate.

This was Michael Jordan…THE Michael Jordan, at the height of his career. He wasn't a legend; he was a God. And I just couldn't be in the face of God. So, I shoved Chet out in front instead. If a bolt of lightning was going to hit someone, it might as well be Chet.

They, Jordan and Scottie Pippin, were making their way through Bears Alley at a good clip and the window of opportunity was narrow. They were on their way to meet up with Lawrence Taylor. Jordan wasn't being aloof or standoffish. It was me. I just froze.

"Chet, you gotta do this! I can't. I just can't." He had an aura, something I had never experienced before. Something they describe in Hollywood as that "IT" factor, and it was just paralyzing to me. Did I make promises to Chet? Maybe.

Chet was stunned. Not that he couldn't get the autograph but that I wouldn't. This was totally out of character for me.

These were the days when people didn't prepare for autographs like they do today. We didn't have anything for Michael to sign. Chet was lucky enough to find an envelope on the ground and fortunately, we had a ballpoint pen.

Chet had no problem with the ask and Jordan signed rather robotically, with no fanfare or ceremony. He simply signed the paper and moved on. Of course, rudely, we never asked Scottie Pippen for an autograph but as good as he was…he was not Michael Jordan.

Today, on that scrap of paper, I also have Lawrence Taylor's autograph. My son's name is Tommy…Junior, to some. Sorry, Chet. And I have never frozen again when it comes to a celebrity which has very often been to the benefit of Tommy

Tommy grew up attached to football. How could he not? And like his pop, he collected the memorabilia that went with it all. For some reason, he was obsessed with the number three. All his jerseys had to have the number three. I had to ask: why?

Joey Harrington. As obsessed as Tommy was with the number three, he was equally fixated on Harrington, the Quarterback for the Detroit Lions. Yes, if you were wondering, he wore the number three.

Harrington was impressive—a poster boy for quarterback fame. Well over six foot tall and good-looking, you simply wanted him to be that all-American success story. And he was. A number one draft pick coming out of Oregon, college PAC 10 offensive player of the year, Oregon Sports Hall of Fame inductee, and College Hall of Famer. Yeah, he came out of the gate running. And there was plenty of hype behind this phenom from the Northwest. But was there too much hope behind the hype? The Detroit Lions were just a lackluster team in the early 2000s and even the promising new prospect couldn't pull them out of the slump. It wasn't long before Harrington was bounced from team to team—Miami, Atlanta, and finally landing in New Orleans with the Saints. Through it all, my Tommy didn't lose his faith or clear hero worship and continued to don that number three—even on his own jersey.

It was 2008, the Bears versus the Saints, I had my usual post with the visitors and Harrington wasn't even a starter for the game. I felt bad when he stepped out of the locker room—having that "oh how the mighty had fallen" feeling. But he couldn't have been nicer. It was as if he remembered all of us standing there from previous visits and previous games. So, I took the moment to approach him.

"You are my kid's hero," I began. Even he looked a little shocked. We both knew that he had never reached the level of superstar. "Every jersey my kid has is a number three because you wear number three. So, I was wondering…if I give him a call, could you say hi to him?"

Ballsy of me, I know. I was not the shrinking loser who couldn't approach Michael Jordan. Of course, Joey Harrington was no Michael Jordan. Still, in Tommy's eyes, he was.

"Absolutely," he returned. "That's cool." He flashed that all-America, things-should-have-been-different smile.

Wouldn't you know, the call went to Tommy's voice mail but that didn't stop Harrington from talking away—giving life advice to Tommy to stay on the straight and narrow and to pursue his dreams.

All the other guys standing there couldn't believe their eyes. Harrington was so cool about the request and so nice with his words, I couldn't thank him enough. He simply smiled and walked away. I secretly think he enjoyed the validation he wasn't getting much of in those days. He was now Michael Jordan in my eyes. As for Tommy, he almost didn't believe it was Harrington on the message. It took some convincing. The convincing worked though; he still has the message saved today.

People liked…well still like Tommy He has a comfort around the players and doesn't react in awe of celebrity. That comfort was something I had to learn and cultivate; his comfort seems to be innate. So, it shouldn't have surprised me that he would have inevitably made his way to the broadcast booth. What did surprise me was just how early it would be and that it would be under the coaxing eye of one of the great players turned broadcasters of all time, Joe Theismann.

We were in Champaign at the University of Illinois temporary stadium digs and I brought Tommy up to the broadcast booth—or what we loosely referred to as the broadcast booth. Being a university stadium of some years old, the booth was not nearly equipped as the high-tech stadiums of today or even of the day for that matter. It was a school announcer booth for all practical purposes and open to the elements at that. So be it, everyone made do. But to a wide-eyed young kid of Tommy's nine years, it was state of the art.

After whisking Tommy around a tour of the suites, we ended up in the broadcast booth where a cameraman took a shine to my precocious kid. He thought he was cute and surprisingly well-mannered. As a reward, the cameraman asked Tommy if he would like to work the camera.

Well, that is like asking a little boy if he would like to drive the firetruck. Tommy couldn't wait to give it a try. The camera was huge, and they grabbed a box so Tommy could step up and see into the viewfinder. Tommy took his newfound responsibility very seriously and no one had the heart to tell him the camera wasn't live.

Just then, Joe Theismann walks in holding a sandwich he has purloined from the neighboring buffet and sees what is going on. This could have gone south very quickly. This was not a place for kids. And as much as Theismann had always been a gentleman to my understanding, talent can be…well…talent. And that doesn't always lend itself to the most tolerant of behavior.

"We've got the new talent to take over my job," he declared.

"Move over Joe," someone shouted back, "they're starting them young."

I can't tell you how proud it made me feel to see everyone having a good laugh along with my son feeling part of the gang…at just nine years old. Yes, I got the requisite pictures of Joe and Tommy working the camera. I had come a long way from the Michael Jordan stammerer and seeing how Theismann and Tommy got along, it seems the intimidation gene was not passed down.

Over the years, I have seen Tommy comport himself just beautifully in the presence of some of the biggest of names. I can't say that is a tribute to me. It's all on him. He's number one in my book…even if he still sees himself as that other number three.

--Tom

FROM PLAYERS...
TO PEOPLE... TO PALS!

There is a fine line between working with people and working for people. When you work "for" them, the relationship is, for the most part, defined. Parameters are in place and boundaries are drawn. There is a proverbial line in the sand. When you work "with" them, you are more likely to create a bond, more likely to fraternize, and more likely to create a lasting relationship. The question is: who defines the difference between what is working "for" or working "with"? The easy way to look at it is, you work for the boss and with a colleague. But in my job, those lines are blurred.

Over the years, I have worked "with" players, coaches, and people in the organization and subsequently, who I call friends and will call friends for a lifetime. Some of the guys I can put in that category include Brian Baschnagel, Jim Thornton, and Steve McMichael. But, by far my closest and most enduring friendship is that with coach Mike Singletary and his wife Kim—with whom, ironically, the friendship formed not at the stadium, not even with him, but through Kim's sister, Mike's sister-in-law Mary Katherine.

My relationship with Mike was, to say the least, professional and perfunctory. Being who he was, he was on my radar as a VIP needing attention when he arrived and left the games. I, in the role of my job, saw to it that he was taken care of in terms of no one bothering him or his family as I escorted him from his transportation to his destination and back again. As I said: professional and perfunctory. That isn't to say we never made small talk and there wasn't a human connection between us. But he had a lot on his mind on game day and I had a job to do and…well… even though I didn't work "for" him, there was that line in the sand. Still, over time, he got to know who I was and only needed to give the eye or a nod and I was at his service or for that of his visiting family to service their needs. Again, it was all very professional. Until Mary Katherine entered the picture.

My main job many years ago was in radio sales and at one point in that career I had been lured to a start-up secular, Christian rock, radio station. Believe it or not, that was big back then. When I arrived at the station. the general manager—with whom I had worked before—had a company-wide meet and greet to introduce everyone as a form of "getting to know you" during which we were asked to talk a little about ourselves. I, of course, talked about my "other" job with Andy Frain and the assignment with the Bears organization. The woman across the room, who, as it turned out was Mary Katherine, promptly spoke up and said, "I know you."

We became instant friends. And it was through her and Kim that I was invited to Mike's house for what started out as the occasional get-together or party, and within a short amount of time, I was as good as a member of the family. Mike is a man of faith and does not choose his friends lightly. So, I am honored to this day to still call him close.

But this is not a story about him and me, it is about how our relationship led to another bonding moment that, yet again covered years and generations. And in this case, it was a family affair.

Every year, my son Tommy and I try to make a weekend out of going to an away game. In the 2009 season, we choose a 49ers game in San Francisco. By then, Mike Singletary had become the head coach of the San Francisco 49ers and he generously offered us two tickets to the game on that particular weekend. The catch for us was, as we were staying out in Oakland with family for the weekend, we would have to come to the city, to the hotel where the team was based, to pick up the tickets.

We got to the hotel early and got sidetracked at the café for a coffee and a snack for Tommy when a guy walks up to the line in which we were standing. He was huge and definitely made a commanding presence. And Tommy, being only twelve years old, couldn't help himself: "Are you a player?"

"Yes, I am," the giant returns gently to my boy.

"Do you play for the 49ers?" Tommy presses.

"Yes, I do."

"What position do you play?"

Now I am intrigued. He answers that he is a tight end. And now it is my turn to be the inquisitor: "Are you Vernon Davis?"

He cracks a big smile and I continue to explain that we are from Chicago, that Tommy is my pestering son, and that I am close friends with Mike Singletary.

The Singletary comment came out of my mouth before I really thought about what I was saying. In a famous dust-up the previous season, Singletary had Davis ejected from the game against the Pittsburgh Steelers. Davis could be a hot head, as plenty in the heat of the game, the heat of the moment, can be. Singletary felt that Davis, in that game, was not playing up to his standards as a coach and benched him from the game. It was a lesson—you are either 100% in…or…as he was about to learn…you are 100% out. Davis grumbled from the bench. And that grumbling turned to some heated bitching. Singletary had had enough and ejected Davis from the field. Harsh…for sure. Not to mention humiliating. The subsequent commentary from Davis has made YouTube fodder to this day.

So, when I mention my relationship with Singletary to Davis right there in that café, I wasn't sure if I had opened the proverbial can of worms. But it was too late now.

Without missing a beat, Davis turned to me and said, "You're friends with Coach Mike? That man changed my life. He completely turned my head around." It was almost as if he was pleased to meet us. It was well documented on how Davis' career had changed since that infamous incident and clearly, he attributes Singletary for that turnaround. (In fact, Davis later is quoted as saying he had wished he thanked Singletary for having benched him. That's how much that moment changed his life. But that's his story to tell, not mine.)

"Can I get a picture of you with Tommy?" I asked and he was quick to oblige—all six foot five of him next to my seemingly scrawny twelve-year-old son.

I met up with Mike to get the tickets and told him of our moment and Mike was quick to point out how much he admired Davis and the changes he had made in his attitude and gamesmanship.

With our moment now a memory, we set out to explore the city for the afternoon. Sure enough, we come across the ESPN store at Fisherman's Wharf and Tommy is quick to eye the Vernon Davis jersey which is now a must-have San Francisco souvenir.

It was a fortuitous purchase as it turns out. Because after the festivities on the field, again thanks to Mike, we were invited back with the team to the post-game barbeque. And who should walk up to say hello but none other than Vernon Davis who couldn't help but spot Tommy wearing his newly bought jersey.

"You know you are gonna money off this merch," he said with a laugh as he grabbed a pen and proceeded to sign the shirt. We continued to chat for a few more minutes and it is all jovial and lighthearted. And we walk away. My impression of Vernon Davis is not one of publicity and YouTube rants but as a genuinely nice and attentive guy. Are we friends for life? Hardly. But it is a moment and a memory. Or is it more than just that?

Eight years pass and Vernon Davis is now playing for the Denver Bronco and my son Tommy is a man of twenty years old. How time flies and life moves on.

It is just one of those games, the Bears versus the Broncos at Soldier Field. I didn't really think much about it at the time. Tommy happened to be there that day as he needed a ride home from work and I had told him to wait at the visitor's locker room area until we could make our way home after the game.

I did what I needed to do and met up with Tommy later, after the game. Tommy and I are making small talk, waiting for time to pass, when Vernon Davis, getting ready to leave the stadium, walks up to the two of us. "How are you doing?" he asks with a smile on his face.

I'm stunned. "You remember me?"

"Yeah from San Francisco. You're friends with Coach Mike."

"Yeah," I stammer, still stunned. "And this is my boy, Tommy." Now six foot one and twenty years old—surely unrecognizable. "He was twelve at the time."

He turns to Tommy and asks how he is doing, and I immediately ask if he'd be willing to take another picture, now eight years later, of the two of them. He readily agreed. And yet again he showed himself to be a true gentleman and not the product of bad publicity.

We went our separate ways after that moment and didn't keep in touch, Davis and I, although I couldn't help but feel that door was open, even just a little, for at least long-term and in this case long-distance communications.

His was the kind of moment that reminds me of what a gift my position has given me…and yes to my brother Chet as well. And rather than being an invisible pawn in the organization, the system of football, you can actually stand out, be noticed, and be remembered. This is never a thankless job even when the thanks aren't always as obvious and can be subtle.

There is a song in the theater musical, ironically named CHICAGO, called "Mr. Cellophane" which laments the story of the husband of Roxy Hart, the hardened murderess of the play. He is a nobody and she has become both infamous and famous. And because of that, while she is making national headlines, he feels invisible to the world, having achieved nothing and noticed by no one. And the song refrain says it all:

Cellophane, Mister Cellophane
Should have been my name, Mister Cellophane
'Cause you can look right through me
Walk right by me and never know I'm there

I mention this because there are people who assume this is who I should be in my job, Mr. Cellophane—at people's beck and call but not really noticed for having done the job. But I believe differently. The craft of my job is to have been noticed in order to make people feel that they have been taken care of in the best possible ways. I never lose sight of the fact that this is not a job, it is a privilege. And, yes, sometimes privilege has its perks.

Similarly, just as people assume I should be the perfect Mr. Cellophane, others frequently ask if I am friends with anybody in the organization or on the team by simple proximity. The quick answer is no. Would I have been friends with Mike Singletary if I had simply done my job? If I had been Mr. Cellophane? Would he have appreciated the effort in the same way? Probably not. It was my relationship with Mary Kathrine that opened that door. But it was being anything but Mr. Cellophane that let me walk through it. Could I have been friends with Vernon Davis? Perhaps. But again, it was my relationship with Mike Singletary that opened that door. This is a good example of how friendships are cultivated. It starts with simple relationships that beget closer relationships which turn into friendships. The game of football is no different from the game of life. You have your players…that end up being just people…who, if you're lucky, can turn into pals.

And when it comes to playing the game, no one is ever going to assume the Ballard brothers to be just another couple of Mr. Cellophanes.

Friendships, and even the ones that come close, are the perks of our privilege.

--Tom

YOU'D THINK THEY DON'T NOTICE...

A Lamborghini! That's what you get when you break a record. Well, it was not just any record. It was Jim Brown's all-time rushing record, and it was not just any player. It was Bears running back Walter Payton—a.k.a. "Sweetness." His career amassing 16,726 rushing yards eclipsed Brown's by over 4000 but it was the day he broke the record which was when he drove off in both infamy…and a new car. And I was at the game when it all went down.

I say I was at the game ironically because it was. It was October 7, 1984, and I did not start with the Bears until two years later in 1986. Although everyone in Chicago had been talking about Payton breaking the record during one game soon, no one was quite sure when that would be. My only way to be there was through Chet.

We had our system. It worked most times but there was no guarantee. I was to be at the press entrance at a precise time. Chet would be on the other side of the gate, but he had a limited window of time by which he could stand around and not look suspicious. So, if I was late or he was called away the whole deal was off.

The deal was this: Chet would identify me in the crowd, point me out to the man who gave out the media passes, and indicate that I was either "Okay" or was under Chet's supervision in one capacity or another. Chet looked very official in his uniform and Chief's hat—no one seemed to question his authority. It all happened rather quickly. I was generally given a pass and let through the gate. Chet would caution me to stand where and only where the media was allowed. This was not all access.

Down by the sidelines, I got to talking to grounds men and the conversation shifted to Walter Payton and breaking the record. He told me that somehow, someway they would make sure the record would be broken during this game. I was thrilled to be there. He went on to say that it better happen because there was a plan—that there would be a surprise waiting for Payton after the game in the parking garage. They were going to replace his car with a shiny new Lamborghini—a little token of appreciation.

The parking situation wasn't valet parking per se, but a couple of guys normally stationed in the garage made sure the players were accommodated in spots as parking was generally limited. On that day, they made sure Payton had his usual spot near the tunnel, closest to the locker room.

The Bears were playing the New Orleans Saints. It took just a six-yard play—a little side-step to the left—for Payton to break the record.

Meanwhile, a little side-stepping was happening off-field. Over the radio, it was said that Payton's car was towed to another obscure parking spot that had been saved earlier in the day and had the Lamborghini delivered to his usual spot. Nothing more was said throughout the game.

After the game, the family and the higher-ups gathered in the parking garage and waited for the man of the hour to emerge. Sadly, I couldn't be there to see his expression when he walked out. Mine was not an all-access pass and even the media was kept outside, not getting access until he drove out. The family and friends wanted to keep his initial reaction a personal moment. Fair enough. This was an extraordinary day and the fans had gathered en masse to show their appreciation. It would have been overwhelming if it hadn't been well controlled.

I eventually saw him drive out and drive into the history books. Just a couple of years later, I would come to know the man I had come to admire on that fateful day.

Payton was as gregarious and affable a man as you can imagine. Always with the jokes. Tipping Chet's coveted "Chief" off his head from behind when Chet would least expect it. Pinching the guy's asses and then scooting away. He'd do anything for a laugh. It didn't matter who you were in the organization, he considered you part of the team. So, I often wondered just who wanted that reveal moment with the car to be personal. It couldn't have been him. He didn't know it was coming…and he would have loved to share the moment with everyone because breaking the record, in his mind, was a team effort. And we were all part of the team. Nonetheless, the moment came, and the moment went. I am sure he was duly appreciative to everyone, there or not.

Some time passed and by then I was also working for a real estate magazine, selling ad space—a sales rep. I worked more in the commercial real estate side. Often, that side of the market would throw elaborate events to wrangle customers and broker viewings. At one such event—a lawn tailgate party—I was asked to attend to represent the magazine and as it happened, they had a "guest of honor" who had a vested interest in the real estate they were promoting: Walter Payton.

For a man who is outgoing and extraverted as he was, when he arrived, he didn't seem to be himself. It's not that he wasn't shaking the requisite hands and smiling that big smile, but he just seemed a little lost like a fish out of water. As he glanced around the crowd, he took one look at me and said, "I know you. From the Bears. Will you sit with me and keep me company?" Of course, I did. It was clear he was uncomfortable with the crowd. I found that part of him fascinating and surprising. With me, he was a totally different person.

He was his charming self, asked about me as much as talked about himself, the game, playing at Soldier Field…even the weather. In case you are wondering, we never did touch on the Lamborghini. There were those who asked for pictures and autographs, and he nicely obliged but for the most part, people left him alone. Perhaps because I was there. I didn't feel like I was being played but I did feel sorry for him. I felt he was being played and he was grateful that I was there, a familiar face, to find security from having to be the product of Walter Payton rather than the person of Walter Payton.

I would have assumed he knew others there of this suit and tie set, otherwise, why would he have shown up, being that uncomfortable in the crowd? Rather he chose me to be his afternoon companion and I'd like to think that it is because we do our job well back at the stadium. We are not faceless, nameless, cogs in the machinery of organization but people who are noticed for our contribution.

Chet was the first to be called "The Mayor of Bears Alley" and many times the answer to many questions was "Go ask Chet," or "Where's Chet?" After Chet left, that baton was passed to me. The Ballard brothers took that responsibility to heart and thanks to moments like that with Walter Payton, we know we were not just there…we were noticed.

--Tom

THE DOCTOR IS IN... SOMEBODY'S POCKET?

Buffalo Bills safety Damar Hamlin goes down on the field after being hit in the right place at the exact right moment and dies from a freak heart attack at 25 years old. And then he is brought back by the medical team on the field. It is nothing short of a miracle.

When Miami Dolphins quarterback Tua Tagovailoa suffers three concussions within two consecutive games, having been put back in the game after the first hit, it is considered outrageous, and the "trainer" is fired. Tagovailoa considered retirement after the incident.

Those were two very different situations, handled in two very different ways. Why? It could go back to the old days when football medicine was considered an oxymoron. No one really knew what to do. There were no apparent rules in place. It was the wild, wild West. And those old days weren't too long ago. Yes, the protocols for player safety have come a long way.

Today, a knock on the head is supposed to lead to concussion testing and potential eviction from the game. Not following those specific protocols can lead to fines and firings as it did in Miami. It is all for the protection of the players, but many say that football is fundamentally a violent game, and if you take away the inherent dangers you take away the thrill of the game, the audience adventure, everything that makes football... football. Players, it is understood, know what they are getting into. But do they?

Time has shown that plenty of players have suffered long-term damage to their bodies and brains that are irreversible due to the relentless pounding they endured over time. And that was only exacerbated by the medical crew back in the day whose job it was to patch them up and get them back in the game. In those days it was all about protecting the investment over protecting the players...or so it seemed.

The Bears had their guy Fred Caito, who was considered a "trainer" which by-passed a lot of questions as to medical qualifications. I'm not saying he wasn't qualified to make medical decisions but being technically a "trainer" smacked of plausible deniability if anything went too far wrong. Protocols in Caito's day when hit in the head weren't MRIs but rather holding three fingers in the air. It wasn't about whether the player could count the fingers but whether they could even identify if there were fingers. Fingers identified...it was back in the game. Shoot 'em up, wrap 'em up, send 'em out. The fans win out. Even the Bears 1988 quarterback Jim McMahon famously attacked Caito by saying: "He couldn't tell a compound fracture from a blister."

But how many players who became addicted to Dr. Feelgood and his pain relief, lost their minds to the lack of proper diagnosis, and could have avoided crippling and painful lives if not been masked by pain pills. Caito was not the only "trainer" in the game. And I can name him specifically because I have plenty of buddies who witnessed the poking and prescribing along the way. As a "trainer," he can comfortably say, with plausible deniability, he didn't know better or, worse yet, it was the industry standard.

I bring this up because one of the greats of football, the Bears' own Walter Payton, was a frequent visitor with the "trainer". Now, it is clearly understood that Payton died too young at 45 from a rare cancer of his liver bile ducts. Questions always loomed as to whether his early pain was masked by the "trainer" and whether he could have been treated sooner and perhaps better by the oncologists he truly needed…but rather spent too much time with the "trainer" and not being treated. Was it too little, too late, by the time he got the help he really needed? And it was all because the "trainer" was doing his thing…while Payton was dying on his watch. Speculation is a dangerous thing. I am not pointing a finger…just holding a finger up to those who participated in those early practices.

So, while you watch a game today and a player is taken off the field surrounded by a medical team for what seems to be an arbitrary scratch or bump, rest assured he is getting the best care on his behalf. It doesn't hurt the game to make sure he's not hurt.

Too many paid a price to make sure today we have standards. It's not just the player on the stretcher, it's the entire game.

--Chet

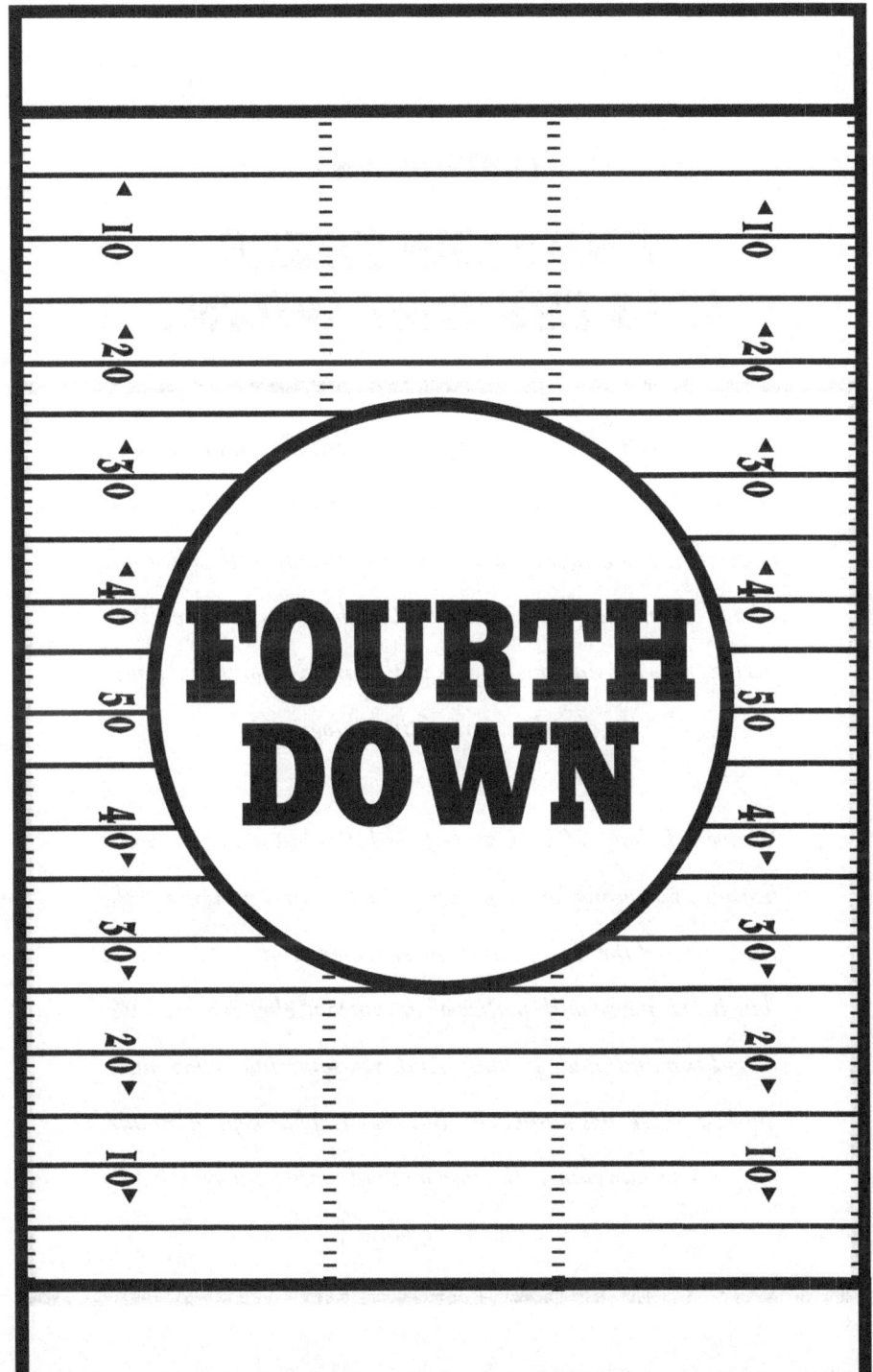

- FORTH DOWN -

AND THEN THERE WAS THE TIME WHEN...

We're asked all the time about moments that made us go "Hmm." There are several and probably even more that we can't remember. From moments with moguls to close calls that could have cost us our jobs, we, the Ballard brothers, stood on the periphery—the sidelines, if you will—and yet somehow found ourselves part of the dialogue.

We were Teflon. We took on responsibility but somehow ramifications for wrong behavior never stuck. Sure, we ignored the rules, crossed the line, pushed the envelope, and broke protocol but it was never with malice or at someone else's expense. We had fun and made friends. And, yes, sometimes when we pushed, there was pushback. But that is what kept us on our toes and on our game. Because football wasn't always the only game being played!

YOU CAN'T ALWAYS GET AWAY WITH IT… AND YET WE DO!

People might say that the Ballard brothers got away with their fair share of antics…and we did. Being the respective "Mayors of Bears Alley" gave us undue, unreasonable, unearned, and unforeseen clout over the years which, yes, we parlayed and pushed to the edge at times. It was nothing malicious and never at the expense of others. We had our close calls and saw a few who weren't so lucky…which sometimes reminded us to stay in our lane—even when that lane was the coveted Bears Alley.

There were always temptations. Whether it was to scoop up discarded player paraphernalia for your own souvenir collection or to let someone in with a wink and nod who hadn't paid for a ticket. Heaven knows, during my early tenure, many friends got the wink more often than they should have and saw plenty of games courtesy of my manning the gate. It is all harmless stuff in retrospect.

Well, when I say harmless…is it also fair to say opportunistic moments factored in at times. You see, I and my friend who works with the equipment folk saw potential in making a few bucks on occasion which may or may not have been above board. Okay, let's just be honest here and say it wasn't.

The Bears players were all allotted tickets for family for each home game. Not every player had family in town, nor did family always show up. Do you see where I am going with this? Tickets were left at the box office simply going to waste with great seats remaining empty. Who would be the wiser if a couple of enterprising young men approached the wanting crowd outside the gate with a pair of prime positions at a bargain price?

So, yes, as if I am in the confessional on my knees, my buddy and I scalped players' tickets…ON OCCASION…and pocketed a couple of extra dollars on the side. It was amazing. No one questioned what we were doing. We looked official in our uniforms. But we were playing with fire, especially being in our uniforms. Putting the legalities of scalping aside—if you can actually call selling house tickets scalping—but doing it in our uniforms was actionable by the company for being fired.

And that was exactly what happened to a colleague of Tom's back in 1987. His was a tragic tale.

He'd been with the company for more than a decade, a solid family man—wife and kids—and took his job and position very seriously. Even the players knew him by name. He too had opportunities and temptations. As he would say, thousands of dollars had been offered to him at times, but he never took advantage.

By 1987, after the Bears' Superbowl win, people were clamoring for freebies and still, he stood his ground. Until this one Sunday. Two men approached ramp 41. There was no one else around. They did the usual begging and asking and for some reason, this time it clicked. Looking around and seeing no one, he palmed the cash and opened the gate. Once inside, he opened his hand to find a one-hundred-dollar bill in it with the words YOU'RE FIRED printed across it.

Tom saw him a few minutes later. He started to cry. His uniform had been stripped of its badges and credentials. It was as if he instantly didn't exist after all those years. He was broken and clearly upset.

"What happened?" Tom asked sympathetically.

He explained the situation and Tom didn't know what to say to Mr. Clean Cut who by chance took the bullet that, on many occasions, was probably aimed at my buddy or me.

When I heard the story, all I could think of was how lucky we'd been…and how cautious we'd better be in the years to come! A cautionary tale for sure.

Unfortunately, we were kids and sometimes we continued to throw caution to the wind. And that wind continued to blow in the opposite direction—benefiting us greatly in the windy city.

--Chet

Actionable offenses come in all forms. Whether you are pocketing a little cash or playing a little pocket pool, getting a little something on the side had a different meaning for different people.

Again, our friend who worked in the equipment department found himself in the thick of things with a couple of gals who wanted to come down into Bears Alley. Although there were protocols in place, back in the earlier days, security was not as strict as it is today. Sure enough, a wink was enough and one of the girls was in. And boy was she in for it. She soon found what she was looking for—one of the staff, again, someone who had been a veteran for years.

Things got a bit amorous, and it wasn't long before the two excused themselves to go down to his car parked in the parking lot below where she let herself go "down below." Now, two consenting adults are… well…two consenting adults. The problem here was, the car was parked directly underneath the open grated catwalk which joined the east and west seats of the north endzone in old Soldier Field. Anyone who walked the catwalk got a bird's eye view through the windshield of the goings on below. And going on, it was.

Complaints were made. Bosses were notified. And that job cost him his job. For him, that really blew. I could go on with obvious puns. But you get the picture. Okay, one last pun. She may have done all the work…but he was the one who blew it.

--Tom

As it is said, let he without sin cast the first stone. I may have paraphrased but I am sure you get the Biblical reference. I too have had my moments, mostly scrounging for souvenirs. I must admit that I am easily persuaded that one man's trash could be my treasure.

Now, technically, we are not supposed to keep the articles we find in the locker room for instance. It is the property of the team—the visitors or the Bears. But do they really want some player's sweaty used hand towel or wristband, socks, or such? Besides, the real gold is in snagging a helmet or jersey, pants or cleats—but they may as well be the holy grail and are swept up by the equipment manager long before the likes of scavengers like me can get into the locker room for a cursory look-see. Sometimes you can get lucky and find the occasional glove or thematic piece that coincides with breast cancer awareness month or something like that. But for the most part, it is a bust.

But my luck was about to turn. It was three years ago, and we were playing the Cardinals. After the game, I waited a sufficient time for the equipment manager to do his thing and gather all the necessary "good stuff" before I entered the locker room. I happened by a garbage can and looked in. There they were as if mana from heaven—pure gold—were a pair of spikes. That kind of gear is never left or most certainly never discarded in the garbage can.

Everybody had cleared out. It was just me and the cleats, waiting to be taken. But how to get them out of the building was another logistical nightmare waiting to be overcome. Just as I was planning my heist, a public relations person from the Cardinals appeared from seemingly nowhere: "What are you doing?"

Being startled only made me look guilty but startled I was, and I couldn't hide it. "I found these spikes," I said nervously. "Someone has clearly left them behind, but all the equipment people have left."

He looked at me suspiciously. He had the 'you-are-going-to-sell-those-on-eBay' look in his accusatory eye. In all my years with the Bears and all the years collecting, I have never sold anything on eBay. So, I knew he was, at least, wrong about that. But the optics didn't look good, me in my security uniform and a pair of contraband cleats in my hands.

He looked as uptight in his suit and tie as I felt. My options were nil. I walked over to him and handed him my unburied treasure. "Perhaps you could return them," I suggested reluctantly. Mea Culpa.

Did I fear for my job? Absolutely. Every visiting team files a report as to how the experience went—everything from the food, to the hotel stay, to how they were treated by the staff at the stadium. It could have easily been noted that a security guard was seen in the locker room post-game looking through the garbage for equipment to take—and worse yet, was found with a valuable pair of spikes in his hand as a result. As I handed over the spikes and he stared me down with that "gotcha" glare, and I knew I was done.

But I wasn't. Nothing was ever said.

I learned a little something about the value of gold that day. I thought those cleats were found gold…only to find them to be fool's gold. What was truly golden…the silence that followed the incident. And for that, I couldn't be richer.

--Tom

PHOTOBOMBING, GUEST APPEARANCE: CALL IT WHAT YOU WILL... THAT'S ME IN THE SHOT!

When you get punched in the face with a television, one could assume you wouldn't develop a love affair with the small screen. But I did. And I did.

The unfortunate face punching happened early on in my career with Andy Frain when I was just fourteen years old and an usher at old Soldier Field assigned to the East corridor making sure people didn't jump the gates to get a free seat in the stadium.

One of the things I learned early on during those days, is that fans—especially those on the losing side—come in with one disposition and leave with another. Fuel that with several beers and the emotions can be incendiary.

Back in the 80s and into the 90s, one of the technological wonders was the portable television. Sony had one that was the size of a medium boom box and ran on batteries, had an antenna for local reception, and a screen that popped up from a spring mechanism from the center of the box. It revolutionized viewing for the fans in the cheap seats. They could watch the game as it played out in the stadium field and catch the replays on the screen in their lap.

At one Monday night game, while Monday Night Football was playing live from Soldier Field, one such fan had the game on, on his portable Sony. I remember the game well as I had turned a blind eye when my pal Jerry Biocic, known as Bio, jumped the gate. I didn't think that his over-the-gate-antic was quite the same offense as the rest of the mainstream maniacs as Bio's cousin was Bears running back John Skibinski—whom later that night, I met in the locker room and that went down as my first official pro player meet-and-greet.

By the time the game ended, I had seen the man with the Sony several times, and he didn't look happy. A losing team fan? As was the normal procedure, we had opened the gates at the end of the stairs so the fans could flow out of the stadium easily. As I mentioned, many of these fans were fueled by emotion, and many more were fueled by alcohol, and the latter didn't flow as easily. My man with the Sony fell into that category. As he got up and walked the corridor, we made eye contact, he and I.

He was a large guy with a full impressive beard, and he made his way toward me. I remember him to be ominous in a way. Determined and aggressive. As he approached, he raised his television and simply hit me in the face with it. No words, just actions. He hit me hard enough to knock me back.

Bio, who was standing next to me, was stunned. "What just happened?"

The man simply turns and says, "Fuck you," and heads down the stairs, out the opened gate, and out to freedom.

I should have thought then and there that this was some sort of a sign and I took it as one: I have the face for television. Perhaps he knocked something into my head but from that point on, I looked for every opportunity I could to make my way in front of the camera or at the very least make my presence known to anyone who would recognize me from a media vantage point. Blame the bearded aggressor but I was smitten with television.

Yes, I can honestly say, I made my way in front of the camera by simply walking in front of the camera during the infamous fog bowl. When no one could see anything, they could see Chet Ballard! Now that took determination.

Mostly my times in front of the camera were carefully executed over-the-shoulder Hitchcock-like cameos behind those meant to be in front of the camera, while being moments of glory for me, were petty annoyances for the professionals working the room. Like the time when the Fox boom mic operator was standing on the sidelines. I had no idea whether or not his mic was "hot" and the broadcast audience could hear what was being recorded over his boom. I crept behind him and screamed over his shoulder "CHET BALLARD! CHET BALLARD!" He was furious. I never did know if my name made it out over the air…but a man can dream.

I never thought of losing my job for such indiscretions. They were moments less of fame and more of infamy, but they were my moments. They were supposed to be all in good fun and the joke was always on me. Not everyone was laughing though.

John Elway for instance.

John Elway was, as they say, "all that" during his time with the Denver Broncos. When he came to Soldier Field it was a media frenzy and I was like a magnet to the cameras. After the game, a presumed win, the national and local media formed a half-moon around Elway for a post-mortem Q and A. This was nothing short of a golden opportunity for me.

I turned to my friend Bubs, who was with me in the locker room and an eager prankster when he wanted to be, and said, "I am going to get as close to Elway as I possibly can and get on camera."

He said, "Watch me. I will signal you as to where you should stand."

The plan was in place. I crept along the semi-circle, and on behind the various officials and people standing around, and found a place near Elway's left side. I looked over to see my navigator flagging me closer to Elway. I shuffled further along. Again, he waved me closer. Again, I shuffled. By the time he was finished, Bubs had me nearly breathing over Elway's shoulder which was fine with me as long as I was in camera shot.

I stood there as Elway fielded question after question. Then out of the corner of my eye, I see it coming. A U.F.O.—a large white ball of an object, heading right for me. Bubs had thrown a large wad of balled-up white tape directly at me and despite my nearness to Elway, it hit me right on the top of my head and bounced off. So obvious was this little stunt, that even Elway was taken aback and stopped what he was saying to turn to me. In fact, everyone turned to me. This was not the notoriety I was looking for, but it was certainly an attention-getter. Nothing was said but I got the message: GET OUT! I made my exit slightly more quickly than my entrance and the questioning continued.

You would have thought moments like that would have deterred me over the years…not so. There were numerous reporters who found a Chet Ballard photobomb in their reporting after the fact, mostly local, but one time I made the big time. Live and national. SUNDAY NIGHT FOOTBALL!

It was back in the day when I still had unfettered access to the coaches' box. Next door and separated by only a window was the broadcast booth. Inside the coaches' box was a live feed television, which meant we got no commercials but rather during the commercial breaks, the feed would show what the broadcast setup would be for the next shot prior to going live.

On this Sunday, my lucky Sunday, it was the Bears versus the Oakland Raiders and I happened to notice that Dick Enberg and Merlin Olsen—the broadcast greats—had positioned themselves with their backs to the window between the booth and the box in which I was standing, meaning the next live shot of them would be looking into the coaches' box. Well, as you can imagine, the temptation was just too great for me.

When the broadcast came back live and the broadcast team began to speak, I leaned into the corner of the window and simply smiled. I damn near had to push one of the coaches out of the way to get my vantage spot, but I didn't care. A producer behind the cameraman frantically began to wave his arms, begging me to move away as clearly, I was in the shot. My goal entirely. I simply ignored him, feigning I couldn't see him.

Little did I know just how recognizable I was. It seems Uncle Fran, the man who was responsible for getting me the job in the first place, and his selected cronies just so happened to be sitting in a favorite watering hole, Ballatores in Country Club Hills, watching the game, when I came up over the shoulder of Merlin Olsen, much to the crowd delight. "That's Chet!" Fran exclaimed. I was now both famous and infamous.

Well, it seems I was more the latter inside the booth…infamous for sure.

The next week, the Fox network was broadcasting and there was a curtain up across the window. The coaches were furious as it was blocking their view of the last corner of the field. Holy hell broke loose. "Chet! Get in there and tell those guys to take down that curtain so we can see!"

Here I was, the guy whose face was the reason for the curtain was now having to go in and tell the broadcasters to take the curtain down. This wasn't going to go over well…and it didn't. I explained the situation, that the coaches couldn't see the complete field and that the curtain had to come down. Fortunately, the Fox crew only knew of the story of some stooge who got in the shot the previous week but not that the stooge was me. They didn't want to take the curtain down for fear of a repeat offense. They simply peeled back the offensive curtain just far enough for the coaches to see and not far enough for me to see…or…the offending stooge, as it were.

Was I a pest, an annoyance? Maybe. In all the time I did my cameos, no one ever complained. I was, after all, the "Mayor of Bears Alley"—armed with my 'Chief' hat and a pair of balls! For the length of my stay at Soldier Field, a camera lens turned me into the equivalent of a moth to a flame. I never got my Andy Warhol's promised fifteen minutes of fame. But the proximity was enough. I had fun and fun trumped fame every time. Ironically, I was less likely to ask for an autograph from a player than to photobomb a press conference. That's me, infamy over posterity.

Now that I think about it Andy Warhol, what's fifteen minutes… when I had years of being close enough.

--Chet

THE ONE THAT GOT AWAY…

I'm not normally an angry guy but I am still pissed off at Phil Collins. I take that back, not at Phil Collins per se, but my moment with Phil Collins…or should I say my wasted moment with Phil Collins.

I am not usually starstruck, but Phil Collins is one of the few people I have always wanted to meet. "Groovy Kind of Love" was my wife Sharon and my wedding song. "In the Air Tonight" is my cell phone ringtone. We have been so lucky as to sit in the fifth-row center for his concert. Suffice it to say we are fans and I border on the obsessed.

In 1986, the Bears played in London and Phil Collins came to the game. As a result, he fell in love with the Bears—became a big fan. And the Bears in return seem to be fans of his, playing of all songs, "In the Air Tonight", in the locker room rundown, pre-game, for what seems like every game back in the day when the coaches fired up the team with a musical medley.

So, the night after his concert—that fifth-row experience--I had gotten the coaches to their boxes and continued walking the corridor along the sky boxes, past the broadcast booth, and along where there was a selection of V.I.P. boxes when out of the corner of my eye, I catch a glimpse. There he is…the Phil Collins. I couldn't believe what I am seeing. So close and yet so far. It is not like I can open the door, walk in, and introduce myself. I start pacing.

Just as I am about to leave, the door opens, and out comes the box attendant followed closely by Collins himself. I'm just standing there staring in disbelief. She gushes and turns to me, hands me a camera, and says, "Can you please take our picture?"

I dutifully do.

As I hand back the camera, I reach over and extend my hand to Collins to tell him how much we enjoyed his concert the night before and how much his music has meant to me and Sharon over the years. He couldn't have been more charming, shook my hand, and left. Could I tell you what he was wearing? No. Could I tell you exactly what was said? No. This was a moment of purely being starstruck. And this is why I am so angry.

It never occurred to me to ask the attendant if I too could have a picture with Collins. I simply handed the camera back to her and let the opportunity slip through my fingers quite literally.

Me! The man who never missed an opportunity to find focus in a camera lens missed the only opportunity he presumably will ever have to be photographed with the one celebrity he idolizes. How could that have happened? I am not prone to regrets. But that is a regret. A BIG regret. I can still see him walking off…into the air, that night. For the man who took every opportunity to photobomb…on the one moment when it counted…I photo bombed!

--Chet

THE ULTIMATE LOSS... WAS NOT ON THE FIELD!

We were in old Soldier Field. We were playing the Tampa Bay Buccaneers and expected to win. The Bucs weren't the best of teams at the time. But a win is a win, and the Bears would take it. Ironically, Tampa Bay was putting up a fight and all eyes were on the field…except for mine. Word had come down from the stands that a woman was having a heart attack. That, in itself, would have been a severe enough situation, but as it turned out, we were being notified on the sidelines that this woman was the mother of one of the rookie Tampa Bay tight end playing on the field. Because she was a player's mother, an ambulance was to be brought into Bears Alley.

It was a logistic nightmare, clearing the Alley, maneuvering the ambulance, and bringing her down. Adding to that, she was not in good shape. She needed immediate attention. Just as importantly, someone had to notify the player, who happened to be in the middle of the field as to what was going on. That was up to the head coach Sam Wyche…who had a different thought. The game was close, and Wyche didn't want to release the player. The decision was outrageous. A close game versus a close call.

I stood there stunned as precious time ticked away. The mother was in the ambulance ready to go while her unaware son was on the field, business as usual. It may have seemed like an eternity, it may have just been minutes, but the call was finally made, and the player was hustled off and into the waiting ambulance.

They made it to the hospital, but she didn't survive. All these years later, I can't help but wonder if the call to the kid had been made sooner, would the mother have made it? There is no way of telling. I never forgot that moment, seeing him getting into that ambulance and those doors closing. I find respite in knowing he was at least there at the end to say goodbye.

Fast forward to the following season and the Bears are yet again playing the Tampa Bay Buccaneers. Again, I am there to greet the visitors as the players' bus arrives. Everyone gets off the bus. That same running back was the last to step off. I recognize him from the season before and the horrendous incident which tangentially bonded us together. I said nothing as we proceeded to the locker room.

Within a few short minutes, he came out from the locker room with roses in his hand. He looked at me and asked if he could go up into the stands. He said he knew the exact seat number where his mother was sitting on that fateful day, and he wanted to place the flowers there. Of course, I would walk him there. I briefly told him I had been there that day and offered my condolences, which he seemed to appreciate.

It turns out, she sat just above the forty-yard line, about twenty rows up. He knew the seat number. When we got there, it was a solemn moment. He placed the flowers in the seat and stood back for a minute or two of silence. I felt awkward being there but somewhat honored as well. I walked down to the bottom of the stairs to let him have some time alone and by the time he joined me, he was teary-eyed. Reasonably so.

I didn't think any conversation was appropriate. I could see this catharsis; this closure was important.

Tampa Bay went on to lose that day. But nothing would top the loss this one player suffered in that stadium a season ago. And it reminded me that it is just a game, football. Wyche took it too seriously that day and took precious time away from a young player and his dying mother.

Over the years I have seen too many tantrums, too many inflated egos, and it is all too much. What does it take to gain perspective? Death? It's just football, folks. It's just a game. Life is not a game…but it is good to remember there are only so many quarters in life like in football before the clock runs out.

--Tom

LIMO SERVICE!

I just drove the golf cart…but you would never know it. They might as well have been limousines the way people clamored for them and coveted a ride in them. Like every golf cart, they were just practical, not posh. Little did I know, in giving me the keys to my four-wheel friend, they had given me the keys to the kingdom.

The golf carts were my idea, at least I am credited with it as I was the one initially racing the coaches on foot to and from the boxes at old Soldier Field—which was nothing short of a hike and a half. During halftime, when precious minutes mattered, that hike ate up the time spent with the team in the locker room. Coaches and teams, in general, complained about the situation but old Soldier Field was built before anyone thought about those sorts of logistics.

I was asked directly if I had any ideas as to how to make the awkward commute from the visitors' locker room, across the field to the coaches' box, any easier. The idea wasn't thought out, it was spontaneous. I had seen a golf cart the groundskeepers used parked in the distance and thought, we should have one or two of those at our disposal. Problem solved. By the first game opener, golf carts were delivered, and I became the chauffeur to the stars.

What I noticed about the golf carts was they became a protective bubble. It was as if they were the hairdresser's chair, the psychologist's couch, or the bar stool gossip. Anything could be said as if it were hermetically sealed with those inside—forgetting or forgiving the fact that a golf cart is open air and the world and the heavens above can hear the goings on. Privy to it all, and included, for the most part, was me. It was as if I was the neutral sounding board, people needed or wanted. It was never a ride; it was always an adventure.

Plenty of coaches wanted my opinion on everything—from what to do in the city while they were here to what I thought about their teams. It was, for the most part, a playful or innocuous conversation that filled the time from here to there. Until it wasn't. Occasionally I was grilled on events going on behind the scenes as if I, the escort, had been elevated to management insider by proxy of the golf cart. I remember it hit me hard when I was hit with the question from some visiting coaches: How long are the Bears going to go on with this Mitch Trubisky experiment?

Trubisky was the Bears' number-one pick as a quarterback in the 2017 NFL draft. That would have been fine, except that his history was… he didn't have a history, and his first year was, let's just say, unremarkable. Players are traded with the stats Trubisky was racking up and with better stats. He could have been, and it wouldn't have surprised anyone if he was except for the fact that Matt Nagy, the new coach was very high on him. Again, why?

Well, it took two years before Trubisky showed any real promise and was named to the 2019 Pro Bowl—as an alternative. But by 2020, the Bears had brought in Nick Foles and the battle for starting quarterback began. In the end, Trubisky was considered a draft pick bust. Whom could they have picked in his place? Kansas City Chiefs Superstar, Patrick Mahomes! Ah, that Mike McCaskey really knows football. That's just an opinion, mind you.

So, when these coaches asked me my opinion I was taken aback. Surely, they had an opinion of their own. Everyone does. That's the one thing I have learned, carting them around, is they all have an opinion of each other's teams. I paused for a moment and then chuckled trying to ascertain if they were looking for actual insider information. It is, after all, part of their job to know what is going on with the other team.

I fumbled my words really, stating something to the effect that Foles had been brought in as a safety measure while Nagy continued to groom Trubisky but, the bottom line was Trubisky still had to show up and put out—that experiments only last until they work or don't. I couldn't have been more non-committal with that answer.

I must say, I do feel elevated when people ask my opinion. Mostly I sat back and listened in the cart. Similarly, I have had silence from owners to players, to V.I.P.s of all sorts. Those are the awkward moments, when I feel they want something but just don't ask—like I should have read their mind. But overall, people are appreciative to be in the cart, getting their limo service—the V.I.P.s especially, because they are there to enjoy themselves and aren't concentrating on the job at hand. And I, in turn, enjoyed them. One, in particular, took me on a ride—down memory lane and I got lost.

By the time Jim Brown got into the cart, he had long since retired from the game but continued to travel with his beloved alumni, the Cleveland Browns, as often as he could. The Bears were playing the Browns and Brown was there to cheer them on. I was there to cheer him on because to say I was a fan was an understatement.

It is hard not to be a fan of Jim Brown, one of the greatest running backs in NFL history who was selected for the Pro Bowl during every season he played, and by 1971 he was an inductee in the Pro Football Hall of Fame. He was larger than life to me and even appeared larger than his 6'2" frame allowed for.

I knew he was coming. We had been notified that he was traveling with the Browns and that he would need some escorting as he was having trouble walking. When I heard he was coming, I must admit, I gushed to my buddies in that fan sort of way and confessed that his movie The Dirty Dozen was one of my all-time favorites.

"I particularly like the scene where Brown runs along the rooftops and he is throwing grenades down," I began but was cut off.

"He isn't on the roof," one of my buddies corrects. "He is running along the sidewalk."

"Look," I defend, "this is one of my favorite movies. I know what I am talking about. He is on the roof, and you are all full of shit."

There were a few eyerolls at that point. And before the conversation could spiral downward, Jim Brown emerged and made his way into the cart. We waited for the General Manager and a couple of others who were delayed. So, I took the opportunity to jump right in.

After the initial gushing and praise of his career—on the field and off—I got right down to it. I mentioned the scene and the rooftop excitement, I so relished.

Without missing a beat, he turned to me and said, "If The Dirty Dozen was one of your favorite movies, you should watch it again. I wasn't on the rooftop. I was running along the sidewalk."

With that, my buddies erupted with satisfactory laughter. Brown gave me a little bump on the shoulder and joined in the laughter. Suddenly he wasn't Jim Brown, the hero…he was just one of the guys.

As a side note, a year later Jim Brown was on the cover of a now-defunct magazine called Sporting News. Again, he had come to town to watch the Cleveland Browns play. Being just one of the guys I now knew him to be, I had no problem asking him to sign my copy of the magazine.

"I know you," he began. "You're the guy from the golf cart." He gave me a look and I wondered if he was going to ask if I had rewatched The Dirty Dozen. I just smiled and he signed his name…being just one of the guys.

Of course, the golf cart isn't always the place to bond. That was the case with Dave McGinnis. McGinnis' association with the Bears is notorious throughout NFL lore. McGinnis was the Bears' head coach that never was.

Oh, he had the job…the only one who didn't know that was him. After the Ditka years, and the Wannstedt debacle, the Bears were desperate for a dynamic head coach to turn things around. They were in negotiations with McGinnis to come over from the Arizona Cardinals. The conversations were going so well that Bears owner Mike McCaskey held a press conference to announce McGinnis had the job. The problem was, McGinnis, who was sitting in a Chicago hotel room at the time, hadn't been given a formal offer. Thinking now the deal was struck and there was no going back, the Bears low-balled McGinnis, and McGinnis, both humiliated and insulted, balked—becoming the head coach, who wasn't. There's that McCaskey prowess again!

I was a little nervous when he got in the golf cart. It was McGinnis up front and two cronies in the back. There are a couple of reporters standing around, joking around. There wasn't tension in the air…more like irony. You know he wanted to beat the Bears, especially on their home turf. And I, awkwardly, was tasked to escort him in order to do so.

When the time was right, we set off. I was perhaps a little heavy on the pedal and as we took the corner out of Bears Alley one of the coaches in the back flew off the cart and onto the ground.

"Man down," McGinnis shouts.

I am mortified, look back, and stop.

McGinnis looks over to me and says, "Is that the plan? To take us out?"

He was joking…yeah…I'm sure he was joking. But in that moment, nothing seemed funny. They even sent a report in, and I was called in to do a formal interview with NFL security on the matter to make sure that, indeed, I had not plotted to "take them out."

In the end, it was determined that the golf cart was at fault, having snapped due to age and disrepair.

By the way, I had gone back to pick him up at halftime. He opted to walk. "I don't want to lose any more coaches," he joked. At least I think it was a joke. Nothing, it seems, is more serious than a man with a joke.

Still, I manned my cart. While some people were an obligation, others were just a pleasure. One who stood out in the pack was Bears place-kicker Robbie Gould's wife, Lauren. They had young kids, so she always arrived late to the games. By then I was inevitably done with transporting the coaches or other dignitaries and I would always make time to give her a cart ride to where she needed to be.

My generosity all came down to her generosity and one word: cookies. She baked… primarily cookies but treats of all kinds. Yes, the law of the job said I couldn't take tips, but a ride could be had for the price of a cookie.

Gould is now with the 49ers, on his way to the Hall of Fame, and my waistline is all the better for it.

A golf cart to me, a limo to others, and a confessional to many more. Who knew that a functional four wheels could take on so many functions and I, its controller turned confidant? I enjoy my time behind the wheel. It gives me insight and invitation without invasion. I am your everyman behind that wheel.

But what I have discovered is the cart is not a luxury as much as it is a necessity. Sure, it provides a purpose, but it also provides a service. Don't underestimate the need to vent, the need to share, the need to explain, excuse, or exonerate. Those few minutes from here to there can be a real thrill ride. So, buckle up…but don't shut up.

--Tom

TAKING A DEEP BREATH... CAUSE SOMETIMES IT STINKS TO BE WITH THE BEARS!

You see the action. You hear the crowd. But imagine if you could smell the game...the grass, the dirt, the sweat. As you can only believe, the locker rooms certainly had a distinctive post-game scent. Smell-a-vision! Would that be sensory overload? Obviously, you can't get a whiff of the action...but there were times when odors came into our lives in pungent ways...ways we may not have expected, putting a little something in the air which changed the dynamic of the moment and gave us a chuckle or a pause. When working within the Bears organization it is safe to say, that on occasion, it stunk.

Maneuvering coaches or V.I.P.s to their necessary boxes seemed easier than you would think. For instance, the visitors' coaches' box was across the field from Bears Alley and the walk to the locker room could take several precious minutes there and back when every minute mattered during a half-time break. Double that or more if they were older or injured.

One day, I happened to eye two golf carts just sitting idle and asked if it would be possible to use them as transport. Oh, I got the usual "there are protocols and paperwork" reaction. But on that day, I simply took the carts as needed and put in a formal request for a later more permanent situation. Request granted. The carts were a Godsend. But I assured the powers that be, they weren't for just anyone.

Danny Trevathan was a star on the team. A stud of a linebacker who also had his share of injuries over the course of his time with the Bears. In his first season, 2016, he ended up on the injured reserve list for a ruptured tendon. Not an auspicious start. In 2019, it was back to the IR with a gruesome arm injury and in 2021 he ended his season, yet again on the injured reserve list. It was during one of those times, Danny and I had our golf cart moment as I wheeled him to a box to join his family to watch rather than play in a game.

For some reason, inside those golf carts, the players, coaches, or whomever, felt free to simply talk about anything. And they did. I heard gossip and plans, predictions and bitching…but never did I have a "bro" moment quite like this.

Danny and I were simply chatting, talking about nothing in particular, when he leaned over and told me I smelled good. The guys, especially the players, weren't prone to complimenting each other in that sort of personal way. I was not prepared for where the conversation might be heading.

"What cologne are you wearing?"

I was taken aback. This hulking linebacker was asking me about cologne! This wasn't the sort of "man's man" conversation I thought I was going to have…but nonetheless, I let him know the brand was a drug store shelf, inexpensive cologne. He nodded.

He had a multi-million-dollar contract from which I could only assume he could afford the best of designer-label fragrances. But he remained fixated on mine.

"It smells pretty good," he continued.

I got him to the elevator, and I am not sure if, on maneuvering off the cart, he didn't take one more sniff, but I must say I would take the compliment over the alternative if he didn't like what he smelled.

Over the years, in and out of the locker room, I witnessed many towel snaps against bare skin, heard off-color jokes, saw pranks and prods, jeers and jabs…guys being guys. Never did I hear anyone talk about such things as skin care, manicures, moisturizers, or colognes—although, I am sure many indulged in those practices.

My moment with Danny was eye-opening. I always thought these guys had to talk about macho bullshit in order to keep up an image, and always be the tough guy. Otherwise, they would lose face on the field. Was Trevathan in the huddle listening for plays or sniffing around for hygiene hints?

But I was wrong. My short conversation with Trevathan only led me to believe that a true man's man is the one who has a whiff of good taste, a nose for new things, and smells the difference between bullshit and genuine conversation. I learned a lot from my that ride that day on the golf cart: a real man's man…doesn't stink.

--Tom

It smelled like shit. Plain and simple. The broadcast booth smelled like shit and legendary game announcer John Madden hadn't so much said it live on the air as much as his expressive face may have let the audience know that something was in the air.

During the time when the team had vacated the old Soldier Field and had yet to build the new Soldier Field, the Bears had relocated to Champaign, Illinois, to the University of Illinois stadium. Fifty miles south of Chicago may as well have been in the heart of Nowhere, USA. This was farm country at its most glorious and the University specialized in an agricultural curriculum. If you are wondering what feeds the luscious land. Fertilizer made from manure.

Not far from the university were the factories which produced that very fertilizer—country gold. But on game day, especially broadcast games, an arrangement had been made to shut down those factories so the offending and often wafting smell of the manure-based fertilizer wouldn't make its way along a gentle breeze and stink up the open-air stadium.

The broadcast booth was hardly state-of-the-art. It was a one-hundred-year-old stadium after all. Open air and high enough to be unobstructed and vulnerable to the elements, with just a table for the broadcasters and bar stools for the talent to sit on, it was particularly susceptible to the offending winds. During this Monday night broadcast, those winds were the winds of war.

Through a series of miscommunications, the fertilizer factories had not shut down for the broadcast and despite the agreement to do so, that would have been fine, except for the unpredicted breeze which began to blow by way of the stadium partway through the first quarter.

To say the smell was pungent was an understatement. From the fans in the stands to my vantage point…you couldn't escape the odor. Without missing a beat, Madden made a comment akin to saying his eyes were watering and added the colorful reasoning behind it. It wouldn't have taken the audience much to connect the dots.

In short, it didn't matter whom the Bears were playing…didn't matter about the action or the score…according to Madden, that night, everyone was in for a shitty game.

Champaign should not be confused with Champagne, the bubbly celebratory wine. Champaign in the eyes of John Madden was just a reason to whine. Being there stinks!

--Tom

The National Anthem is a sacred tradition at the start of every game and picking the talent to perform and the performance itself is no afterthought. And when it came to the playoffs, more thought went into every detail of the game as a performance piece…including the Anthem. At this championship game, the Eagles versus the Bears, it was decided the National Anthem would be a highlight sung by Gloria Estefan and with the added attraction of a fly-by from an actual bald eagle. An eagle for the Eagles. Clever, at least on paper.

The plan was as Estefan was singing, the eagle would fly from the top of the stadium to join her with a podium landing. Easy enough for the trained bird who had done this on many occasions for many occasions. A trained professional. Dramatic. Impressive. What could go wrong?

Prior to the game, there is an auxiliary locker room close to the referee's locker room which is only really used for V.I.P.s or in this case as an artist's waiting area. It is a relatively small space with just a few locker stalls lining the wall and a shower. It had a television and a few creature comforts, more than say an eagle would need, as that was where he was being kept. Estefan was on her own. The bird, on the other hand, got a room of his own.

While in there, the handlers fed the ravenous eagle. You can imagine what that feast consisted of—rats for the most part, which the eagle devoured eagerly. There is something to be said about eating before a performance. Traditionally artists and performers don't. And this, as it turned out, should have been one of those times.

After his hearty dinner and before the performance, the eagle was taken out to Bears Alley while it waited to get into position. The bird was impressive, to say the least. Its body was about the size of a young boy and its wingspan stretched several feet out either side. It seemed everyone wanted a look, and several wanted a picture with this beast.

Despite the bird being perched in the middle of the alley, the usual pre-game activity continued all around. All the referees were now out in the alley while waiting to go out on the field. Perhaps it was all the people. Perhaps it was all the excitement. But the eagle had had enough and proceeded to let loose and drop the largest load any of us could believe would drop from an animal, let alone a bird. Taking into consideration what the eagle had just eaten, and digested, the smell was horrendous. Acrid. Rancid. And worse yet, wafting quickly, everywhere. Like how cigarette smoke attaches to things like clothing and hair, the stench was bleeding into the refs' uniforms. Yes, it was that bad. No one and nothing was saved from the permeating poop.

There was a scramble as to who was responsible for cleaning up the wreaking mound. And the more it sat there, the more it stunk. People were trapped, not able to go out to the field yet. And the more they stayed, the more they were tainted. The only people laughing were the handlers who apparently had seen this little circus act before.

By the time everyone got to the field, the damage was done. Everyone smelled like putrid poop.

The Anthem went off without a hitch. The eagle did what the eagle did best and thank God for a breezy day, the stink on the refs quickly dissipated. It was glorious to have the symbol of American freedom perform for an appreciative audience…never to have been privy to the pre-show…shitters…er, I mean…jitters.

You can say what you want about how tough it can be dealing with the egos of professional sports players, coaches, and team workers. But I now know that is nothing compared to these show business divas… they just stink.

--Tom

Saving face? That's hardly what my buddy had in mind one afternoon when we decided to prank the official timekeeper for the NFL. We didn't do this arbitrarily. We didn't pull pranks often. This guy deserved what he had coming. And on this day, for this game, the opportunity came our way.

By way of background, the referees have a strict uniform policy. You can't cover up their uniforms under any circumstances. So, for instance, if it is bitter cold, they can't wear a jacket over their striped shirt or to cover their faces which could block our ability to see them make a call. That is why, on those rare days of extreme weather, they layer below with long underwear and sweaters, etc., underneath the uniform to keep as warm as they can. And the inside trick to protect their faces from the elements? They smear vaseline over their skin to protect it from bitter cold or biting winds.

The lines people, on the other hand, don't have such rules. Those people include, for instance, the chain holders who mark off the first down measurements. Also included among those who can bundle up and keep warm is the aforementioned timekeeper, who, on the day in question lauded over the others his ability to do so.

I was in the locker room with my buddy when the timekeeper pulled out a rather elaborate and clearly expensive new face mask—much like a scuba mask: skin-hugging and designed to keep the skin warm in frigid conditions. It was brand new, still in the package, and he was waving it around for all to see as if to say: "Suckers…suffer out there. I won't be."

He bragged about how it was the best thing on the market and went on with detail after detail. It was obnoxious. I felt for those unable to have that choice and would, indeed, have to "suffer" out there.

Mercifully a meeting was called, shutting him up, and everyone left the room. It was a standard meeting, nothing out of the ordinary but it gave us an opportunity I didn't see coming. My buddy turns to me and says: "How about if I take that mask out and take the nose and mouth area and I rub it all around my balls and between my ass cheeks and then put it back in the package without him knowing it?"

No one deserved it more and I gave my blessing, not completely sure that he could pull it off or in time.

Sure enough, my buddy pulls the package out of the timekeeper's locker and manages to slide the mask out without so much as breaking a seal on the previously unopened packaging. Houdini! He drops his pants, goes to work, does as promised, and again, replaces the mask in the package as if it has never been opened.

Meetings are over and the timekeeper comes back in, finishes dressing, grabs his prized mask, and heads for the field.

You know we made it back to the locker room by the time of the next chance everyone would be there, and sure enough in storms our guy with the mask in his hand. He throws it across the room in a fit of disgust and anger. "This thing smells like shit!" he declares to everyone and no one in particular.

I had to walk out before I blew our cover but hadn't gotten far enough away before I see him storming from the locker room, heading for the field…no mask, no cover…NO SHIT!

How did he put it: Sucker…suffer out there!

    Getting a little frostbite…like the rest of your co-workers…now that stinks!

--Chet

GOING LOW...
AFTER MILE HIGH!

Cheerleaders, they're an institution in sports…right? Well, not everywhere or for everyone. The Buffalo Bills, Cleveland Browns, Green Bay Packers, New York Giants, Los Angeles Chargers, and the Pittsburgh Steelers don't have cheerleaders and neither do the Chicago Bears. But that wasn't always the case. The Honey Bears were a crowd favorite for Chicago Bears fans for nearly a decade and then disappeared as quickly as they arrived. Speculation has surrounded why that happened ever since.

Let's start with how they arrived. With much fanfare in 1976. They were the brainchild of owner George Halas who saw the success of the Dallas Cowboys Cheerleaders and thought a similar gimmick would draw fans. Imitation is the sincerest form of flattery it seems. But the Honey Bears were a force unto themselves. Though they were an instant hit.

The troupe of 28 girls made the staggering fee of $15 a game which was raised to $20 by 1985. Still, so popular over five thousand girls auditioned. And the audition was grueling with the girls having to show multi-talents such as the ability to sing as well as dance. They appeared on television shows and even in ads for products like Vidal Sassoon hair care.

Although they were a hit, when Halas died in 1983, heir Virginia Halas McCaskey was reputed to declaring she wanted the Honey Bears out believing them an insult to women and publicly referred to them as "sex objects." Having to honor their contract to the end of the 1985 season, the Honey Bears had their final performance at Superbowl XX at the Superdome in New Orleans.

Despite attempts to bring them back, Virginia McCaskey has let it be known that as long as she owns the team there will not be cheerleaders. On January 5, 2023, Virginia McCaskey turned 100 years old and there are still no Honey Bears.

McCaskey's wish is the public excuse for the demise of the squad. We're expected to buy into that with a shrug of the shoulders and a collective "Oh well." Even though it seems that it is just a philosophical issue… was it?

I have heard otherwise.

Word has it that the Honey Bears were quite the honey pots. And the reason for their departure was like honey…sticky.

At this point, it is worth mentioning Otis Wilson. Wilson was selected in the first round of the 1980 NFL Draft by the Chicago Bears as a linebacker who along with the linebacking trio of Mike Singletary and Wilber Marshall helped the Bears to win Super Bowl XX. Just for fun, it is also worth noting, he was a featured soloist of the "Shuffling

Crew" in the video The Super Bowl Shuffle in 1985. Wilson was not the shy type.

Why do I mention Wilson? Word, if the word can be trusted, is that on the chartered flight back from New Orleans Wilson invited a few of the Honey Bears to the back of the plane along with some of the other males flying high to enjoy their company. One thing led to another and before you knew it…oh Honey! Going low while mile high.

The next thing you knew, the Honey Bears were fired. You can't have the Honey Bears' squeaky-clean image tainted with such a story. Because rumors, like honey, sticks to everything. It was easier to get rid of them than to deal with them.

No, I was not on the plane…but a pal was. Do I trust his word, or do I believe that a 100-year-old prude is just a feminist at heart? It's the bare facts versus the Bear facts. You must be careful if you poke the proverbial bear. Like I said…Honey! It's sticky!

--Chet

WAS IT WORTH IT?

150 head coaches. 480 coordinators. That doesn't include the players, various V.I.P.s, and the rest of the teams' support staff along the way. That's who I met over the years. George Mandich, the head of NFL security for Chicago, made sure of it with a simple sentence: "This is Chet Ballard and he is my man." And that gave me all the clout I needed to be associating with some of the most powerful men in the NFL. Mandich gave me a calling card. It was up to me to use it.

What were you thinking Uncle Fran, back in the day in that bar when I was just 14 years old and you asked if I wanted to work for Andy Frain? Not that it was as much a question as it was a mandate. You, Fran, were several drinks into the day and I was too young, too naïve, to know that your idea seemed more pie in the sky, than based in reality. What was I going to do for Andy Frain? I didn't even have my driver's license. What did you know that I didn't? Did you know that by 17, I would be fraternizing with such big game, big wigs? It wouldn't be long after that that peers and personnel would be calling me the "Mayor of Bears Alley"…and at that point, my ticket was stamped. Did you know that one conversation, that one idea, would change my life?

I didn't come from a culture of knowing how to take advantage of opportunities. My parents were little more than worker bees and didn't aspire to more than the notion of "a roof over your head and clothes on your back" as defining success. Uncle Fran was a mover and shaker, but his dealings always seemed cloaked in some sort of whispered give and take and sealed with a drink and a handshake rather than a contract. Even in my young years, I could figure out that Uncle Fran was an original—not the norm—and made the rules, didn't follow the rules. But he made things happen and with a wink and a nod, I was in at Andy Frain. At this point, it was mine to lose.

From that moment on, I lived what could only be called a charmed life. Whatever I did, I was the first. I developed and defined a job that basically didn't exist. And if there is a line that encapsulates my life with the Bears, it's: "Check with Chet." It was the staff mantra. It was as if they couldn't make a move without me. In reality, who the hell was I?

I didn't have the guidance of Uncle Fran every step of the way, nor the wisdom…but somehow by osmosis I had his creativity and ability to adapt. I made my position, didn't wait for instruction but rather let them know what I was up to. Somehow it worked.

Starting so young, it never occurred to me that I could accomplish so much and it is only in retrospect that I truly understand what that means. I learned what a team really consisted of, even if my idea of teammates was better defined as cronies. Those boys who turned to men along with me are still in my life and together we have a lifetime of hi-jinx and dodged bullets to show for it. If you think that wasn't in Uncle Fran's plan, think again. Bonding with lifelong friends could not be an accident.

Yes, I learned along the way. Mine was an education not found in textbooks but in real-life situations. I was attending the University of Soldier Field and I was determined to graduate at the top of my class. I made business assessments, personal judgments, evaluated crises, and solved problems. I learned to be the "Mayor" and that with a title, even one that is made up, comes responsibility. I had to step up or step out. Doesn't that come with any job? But this wasn't just any job, I had to continue to carve a niche and make it my own. And, oh yeah, along the way I grew up.

Occasionally I would pause. No one would see me and no one really knew what I was up to—after all, I had a virtual free run of the stadium. I would find a moment and think of Uncle Fran. Had I done him proud? Will I continue to do him proud? It was as if his reputation mattered more than mine. Hell, was I really thinking of my reputation with some of the antics I and my cronies were getting up to and away with?

In fact, my reputation was solid. The Ballard name meant something—possibly from what I learned from pure observation: respect others and they will respect you.

The thing about Uncle Fran was for a man who was the life of the party, who owned the room, a raconteur, and a business hustler; you didn't need words to prove yourself. We spoke very little about the actual job. Actions spoke louder than words and he was simply proud of the fact that

I had carved a place for myself, independent of everyone and it was working. Mission accomplished. It was up to me to reconcile that I had done enough. It took me years to understand that as long as I was happy…he was even more so.

I couldn't be more grateful for the time I spent with the Bears, the lessons I learned, the people I met, the experiences I had, and the memories made. I would not have made my significant life decisions without standing on the foundation I built with the Bears. And yes, it comes down to thanking just two people: Uncle Fran and George Mandich…if I weren't so mad at him.

As much as Mandich did me a solid all those years ago by bringing me under his wing and giving me the launching pad to define my entire career with Andy Frain and the Bears organization, remember the old adage: there is no such thing as a free lunch. Mandich brought me in, yes, but to do his job. He handed me responsibilities to simply get them off his plate. Okay, who is a 17-year-old to complain? The problem was when the team won the 1985 Superbowl and Superbowl rings were being given out to support staff for a job well done, Mandich got one for the job I was doing. To this day, I want the damn ring!

I know it seems like a petty want after a lifetime of rewards, but it does represent an actual symbol of team recognition. I laugh a bit when I think about it and know that if Fran were here, he'd probably figure out a way to get me the ring. Still, I have memories that are worth their weight in gold and lasting friendships that are worth even more.

But ironically not getting the ring was a learning lesson unto itself. It made me re-evaluate all of the Bears' years. A ring is just an object, a thing but an experience can be life-altering if you let it. To that end, perhaps that is what I have taken away and cherished the most. The things I couldn't hold, are the things I hold on to the most. I may not be jeweled but the Bears experience was nothing short of a lifetime of riches.

--Chet

It was 2020 and the NFL was celebrating its 100th Anniversary. Each franchise was left to its own accord as to how it would honor the milestone. The Chicago Bears opted for a 2-day fan appreciation event at the Rosemont Convention Center—with its 6 halls and 30,000 square foot lobby—it was preparing for somewhere close to 40,000 attendees. They were even going to parade out Virginia McCaskey, who was nearly as old as football itself, to greet the supporters.

I knew it wasn't business as usual, orchestrating security for the 40 past and present players who would appear to sign autographs over the course of the two days. You couldn't help but feel a part of sports history. What I wasn't expecting to experience were the feelings this event would conjure up and the recalled moments from the reunions and reconnections. I didn't realize that while I was attending a moment in sports history, I was already so much a part of sports history. And that would come flooding back.

The meet and greet part of the event was set up whereby the players all had one hour to sign autographs as the fans filed in, having won the privilege to meet the players by lottery. My job for those two days was to orchestrate the comings and goings of the players and to keep things organized with the flow of fans. It was a tall order and it had to run like clockwork.

That's where I had come to in my career. I was "that" guy, the guy you could rely on to make these logistics happen with no one to worry about the details. I felt proud that I had been given this responsibility for such a monumental event in NFL history but I still had to remind myself that I wasn't there by accident.

It wasn't always easy for me, a simple guy, to take the credit I deserved. I was just doing my job…right? As such, I probably missed opportunities over the years and along the way that I not only had grown to be qualified for but could have parlayed into major industry success. So be it. I am not a man prone to regret.

Still, as the players filed in during those two days, I couldn't help but have a bit of a personal epiphany. These people were in my life, some in more important ways than others. But if they were in my life, I had to have been in theirs, even tangentially. That made me think of just what a team is and what is my place in it. I finally felt like a Bear and not just a secondary employee, an Andy Frain.

There were so many familiar faces, faces who were friends. Friends like: Mike Singletary, Tom Thayer, Brian Baschnagel, Jim Thornton, and

Kyle Long—and we greeted each other like old friends. There were other players who all took a moment to acknowledge me for being part of the team, even in its periphery… reiterating my new mindset. Players like: Khalil Mack, Brian Urlacher, Lance Briggs, and "Peanut" Tillman—who was famous for the "peanut punch" which opportunistically made for more fumbles against opponents than any other player and today is an offensive move used by players throughout the NFL.

Then there were the members of the 1985 Superbowl championship team, Jimbo Covert, Kevin Butler, and William "The Refrigerator" Perry—all of whom simply reminded me of the glory and the legacy of the Bears. It was a magical two days filled with cheers and tears as I reflected back on my nearly four decades with the team—my team.

The things I'd seen, the things I'd done, the people I'd met, and the hands I'd shaken—I look back not just to cherish the memories but also with awe at the opportunity handed to me by my brother, and to my brother before me, by Uncle Fran. Fran saw what we could not all those years ago—to turn simple boys into polished men. His vision, as I see it now, was not to have us work with the team but to be on the team. And we succeeded by carving careers, a needed niche, unique to the Ballard brothers that endeared and endured.

This was a privilege and a passion, not just a position, and not just working with the Bears but with the visitors and franchises from all over the NFL. It has made me a better person. It educated this simple man on how to work with people and understand business but, moreover, taught me to be a better person to others by seeing how teams can be family. And I was able to do it all--to work, share and grow with the two most important people in my life: my brother Chet and my son Tommy.

Along the way, we had some fun...too much fun...and saw and heard some things that maybe we shouldn't have. I could have and maybe should have been fired for some antics and rewarded better for other achievements. I am proud of the fact that the Ballard name has a solid reputation—relationships were cultivated and bridges weren't burned. That is as solid as it gets. It is called legacy.

They say a person has everything if they have two solid friends—you know the kind of people in your life that you can call at two in the morning when you are really in trouble, and they will be there for you. I think if it weren't for my time with the Bears and the relationships that weren't as much cultivated as they were grown organically, and the maturation of the man I grew into, I wouldn't have those two friends. Instead, I have many more. For that alone, if you ask was it worth it? What do you think?

Four decades with 'Da Bears'...people always ask me, where's the best seat in the house. I always tell them, I couldn't tell them as I was always on the sidelines. But I will tell you, it is not the view that matters... it's how you see the game.

--Tom

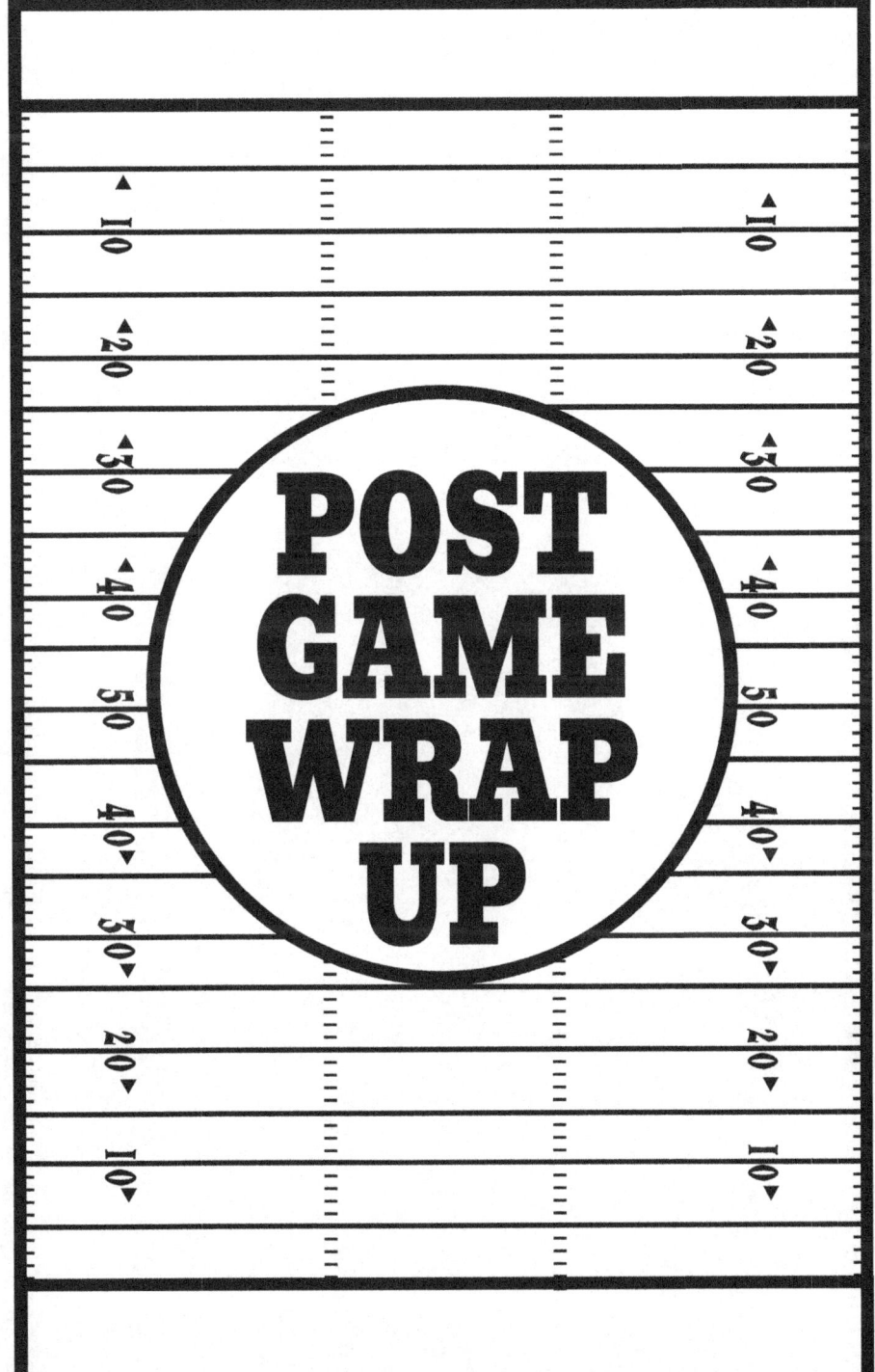

BUT I'M A FAN TOO...

What made this job great was that I was…am…a fan of the Chicago Bears. For two decades, before I hung it up, I got paid to be there on the good days and the bad to cheer and, yes, jeer with everyone else. Paid for the privilege of being a fan. But even I got tired. Tired of being a fan.

How many times could they lose? How many times could I get my hopes up, just to have them crushed? I drove a considerable commute—two hours each way—to the stadium every weekend and that commute grew longer as the team became sadder during my later days. And in my opinion, it all came down to one man. Dave Wannstedt!

Head coach Wannstedt was hired in 1993 to replace the legendary Mike Ditka and to say his tenure was tumultuous may be an understatement. In my opinion, and it was just my opinion as a fan at the time, he was clueless about managing football players. And it seemed to show. His record stands for itself. He led the Bears to only one post-season appearance in six years. That's not impressive if you're a fan. In fact, it's rather depressive.

My wife Sharon and I were thinking about a life change, moving to Florida. It was a long time coming and there were plenty of circumstances leading up to it. One of the things keeping us close to Chicago was the Bears. Wannstedt, his coaching results, and the grind of the job were quickly beating the stuffing out of that teddy Bear. You know what they say, get out when it is no longer fun. Under the Wannstedt tenure, the Bears were no longer fun. Maybe it was bad timing but it seemed to me that if I had to point a finger at something or someone, Wannstedt was literally making me quit my job. So, in 1997 we made the move.

By 1998, Wannstedt was out—ousted on one of the more infamous days in football history when five NFL coaches were fired on the same day. I couldn't say I was surprised by his dismissal. By then, it was too late for me. I, too, was gone.

I may be gone but a Ballard brother, Tom, stayed on for another 20 years keeping the "Mayor of Bears Alley" a family institution. You would think I would have put it all behind me. But you can't and I won't. I had packed up my fond memories and great appreciation for all my years and moved south but will always have a piece of my heart back in the heart of Chicago. I have a room in my house devoted to the memorabilia and my cheeky and cheerful stories still entertain over cocktails.

But the ghost of football past continues to haunt me. Like something out of Dickens, I have run into Wannstedt. It was 2005 and Sharon and I were returning to Florida from a visit back to Chicago. As we were making our way to baggage claim, I looked forward and I saw him. Wannstedt, it turns out, lives just about a forty-minute drive down the coast from us in Florida and he happened to be on the same flight.

"I'm going to say something to him," I tell Sharon.

"Oh no you are not," she cautions.

"I have to…"

"No, you don't!"

"Yes, I do. He ruined the Bears for years for me and damn it, I am going to tell him so."

I was emphatic. Just how many chances do you get to confront your demons? In my mind, he was my demon. Yes, I was being irrational. Yes, I was acting like a petulant child. But he was the living, breathing bad memory in a lifetime of only good. Somehow, on behalf of this fan, this contributor, this team participant, he needed to be held responsible… right? Sharon was the voice of reason, fortunately.

"Just keep walking," Sharon insists. She grabs my arm and pulls me back into the aisle.

I just wanted to say: "Thanks for f**king up the Bears for so many years!" That's all. Was that too much? Was it even fair? It's a team sport and the team, from the management to the players has to hold some responsibility. But all I could see at that moment was the man I wanted to blame. I wasn't going to make a scene or throw a punch. I just wanted to state what I felt was obvious—it all lands on the shoulders of the head coach.

Fans know these things and the people who are responsible need to be accountable to the fans. I know he got fired. But being fired isn't personal, it's business. I wanted him to know that what he did was personal to the fans. And I am a fan too. You just don't get an opportunity like this, and I wanted my moment.

In retrospect, I have to thank Sharon for holding me back because I know whether I am a frustrated fan or the former Mayor of Bears Alley, I am a bigger man than to get into a pissing match in the airport with that man who already paid a price of his own. Did I really think that he would recognize his own flaws? How many of us do? My momentary outburst would make me the crazy one and he the victim. And the last thing I want to do was make him seem like a victim when it is the hundreds of thousands of Bears fans who were the victims during the dark years.

Today, occasionally, I see Wannstedt hawking the merits of a random local business on some low-market local commercial, and I think to myself "Oh, how the mighty have fallen." But he hasn't fallen. Today he is a respected commentator back on Chicago local television—known as the "Beloved Wannie." You can forgive…but how did everyone forget? Oh, well! Still, I find solace in seeing how the Bears have reclaimed respectability over these same years.

Hell, if Chicago can forgive their "Beloved Wannie", I can certainly shake off the remainder of any long-held animosity. Time has healed plenty of my wounds. I look back with only the fondest of memories of my time with the organization and not with the bitterness that Wannstedt may have momentarily inflicted.

Although I must also admit, I go through my days with the assurance that he lives only forty minutes down the road. You never know if our paths may cross. I didn't have my say on that day…but one day, who knows? Now that I think about it, mouthing off may just be more catharsis than crazy after all. Today, I may explain that I am better more than bitter for having been there and that we both should all be grateful for having been a part of it. I just may be a little more colorful when I explain that.

So, when that day comes, on behalf of all Da Bears fans…Sharon, block your ears.

--Chet

Made in the USA
Coppell, TX
30 December 2025

67538702R00167